# ONE DAY AT A TIME

## across NC

A Solo Run/Walk Behind a Baby Jogger

DAVID FREEZE

Published by:
Walnut Creek Farm Publishing
China Grove, N.C. 28023

Designed and cover photos by Andy Mooney

ISBN 978-0-692-16429-7

# FOREWORD

L eave it to two invincible forces to carry out a challenging mission.

When David Freeze announced in early 2018 that he was going on a cross-state run in memory of the Salisbury Post's former sports editor, it made perfect sense.

David has become famous in our part of North Carolina for his solo, cross-country bicycle trips. Over the five summers from 2013 through 2017, he logged more than 15,000 miles traveling in 45 states, and early this year he pedaled through a couple more. But this book is not about cycling.

It's about David's first love, running, and a friend we all thought would never stop running, Ed Dupree. Though Ed worked at the Post for many years, the people who gathered to celebrate his life last November spoke more often about his unstinting support for young athletes — and his determined running. Ed vowed in 1993 to run at least a mile a day, no matter what, even if it was just to run circles around the newsroom as the clock ticked toward midnight.

Ed's running streak finally ended in 2017 at 21,957 miles, halted by a pulled muscle. He died several months later of a rare form of leukemia he'd been sparring with for years.

Ed's running went well beyond that streak, as sportswriter Mike London reported in the Post. "He recorded every mile he ever put behind him and ran at least once in all of North Carolina's 100 counties. All told, he ran 41,093.5 miles. He completed 13 marathons."

If Ed was the epitome of persistence, David Freeze has been its first cousin, covering miles upon miles of the nation's highways in pursuit of new destinations. He has cycled up steep inclines, through bone-chilling cold and under energy-sapping heat. He sets goals and reaches them, and neither rain nor sleet nor rumble strips will stop him.

So when Ed suggested in his last days that David try running across the state — something Ed had wanted to do — David had a new mission.

What follows here is the story of that 647-mile trek. While David was a veteran at bicycling long distances over the nation's highways, he found the going very different on foot, running behind a baby stroller designed for joggers. Many a person stopped to offer help and was probably surprised to find David was pushing a load of supplies, not a baby.

As he did on his cycling trips, David reported his adventures to the Salisbury Post at the end of each day, to be shared with readers in the next morning's paper. It turned out to be a 23-day trip, faster than you might expect. Ed had asked if David could run 10 miles a day. Some days on the Murphy-to-Manteo run, David and the baby jogger covered more than 40 miles.

David is known for his endurance, determination and unrelenting optimism. Though he didn't always turn in at night relishing the next day's journey, he found ways to make the best of challenging situations. Aches and pains were endured; annoyances morphed into anecdotes. He can make light of bad drivers, a debit card that gets used in Kenya and smoke-free rooms that don't include chairs. But he takes his pineapple milkshakes seriously.

It takes a special person to set his sights on a spot way beyond the horizon and go for it with everything he's got. In a way, this is a story about two such men, both known for setting audacious goals. David covered the miles on foot, and Ed's inspiration was with him every step of the way.

— **Elizabeth Cook**
*Editor, Salisbury Post*

# ACKNOWLEDGMENTS

As I have said many times before, the team of fine folks who contribute to these adventure books are the real stars. I am the fortunate one who gets to go see the country, meet fellow Americans and hear their stories.

Once again, that team of contributors includes Salisbury Post Editor Elizabeth Cook who provides the foreword. I consider Elizabeth to be the best writer that I know. Kathy Chaffin is back for her second book as the chief editor, and the man who puts it all together is the Post graphic designer Andy Mooney, who also shot the cover photos. This is a wonderful group of professionals and friends who I have been able to count on each year. The easiest part of all of this is riding the bike and running the road. I can't wait to get out the door to do these trips, but writing the book afterwards is much harder work.

At home and on the farm, I again had the help of farm manager Sammy Freeze and the best neighbor of all time, Ollie McKnight. My daughters, Amber and Ashley, and their husbands, Jamie and Dale, were big supporters as well.

Friends and businesses who also deserve special recognition for their support were the Salisbury Post, Father and Son Produce with Tim and Linda Hoffner, Accelerate Therapy and Performance and Delaine Fowler, Ralph Baker Shoes and Ralph Baker, Jr., Gentle Dental and Dr. Tanya Williams, Gear for Races with Luis Villareal, Vac and Dash and Peter Asciutto, Skinny Wheels with Eric Phillips, plus Darryl Fisher, Jim Duncan, Tim and William Deal, Crystal Karriker and Wayne Crowder.

Suggestions, contributions and prayers along the way from so many readers have made each trip better and more rewarding for me. To the many who reach out with your support, you help keep me going. With each trip, I hear from a consistently supportive group but always am amazed at how many new readers join in and the far-reaching responses. Those messages are the best treatment for sore legs, and they keep my spirits flying high.

Thanks to all the Dupree family members who were genuinely excited about my run across North Carolina. Ed was a great friend, and I am grateful that he proposed the idea of this adventure. I thought about him constantly and wish that he would have realized his dream of crossing the state on foot.

And finally, I have never run or rode a single mile without God's comforting presence. And I never will.

# INTRODUCTION

When I am home for any extended period of time, several things happen. I get restless and start searching for more opportunities to travel, incorporate some extended adventure and go somewhere new. After long cycling trips over the previous five years, I realized how much I love endurance cycling. I had just finished a summertime ride from Washington to Wisconsin by way of Idaho, Montana, North and South Dakota, Iowa and Minnesota. That ride totaled almost 3,000 miles and 36 days across the Great Northwest.

To top that off, I had plans in place to ride for a possible 10 days on the Inner and Outer Banks of North Carolina. I wanted to do this trip for several years and had been researching the route for more than a year.

That was September of 2017. My plate was full just like I want it to be. I heard that one of my running friends, Ed Dupree, who had a 24-year plus streak of running every day, had just stopped. His daughter, Allison Adams, told me that Ed was in the hospital, and I went to visit him. While he appeared fine, Ed told me that he may have just months to live and that his best hope was an experimental treatment. I struggled to believe that Ed couldn't beat this, simply because he had always set huge goals and accomplished them. Some of them were goals that required lots of planning and sometimes years to accomplish. Surely a simple blood disease couldn't take him out.

But Ed was serious about his life expectancy, and he told me that one of his biggest goals still hadn't been achieved. He and I always talked running, but this time was different. Ed's tone took on a serious quality that I hadn't heard before when he asked me to consider running across North Carolina. He told me the estimated distance and a little bit about his own plans to do it. Ed said, "I didn't get to do it, but you could."

When I left the hospital that day, I couldn't get the thought of this adventure out of my mind. I hadn't told Ed that I would do it, but I did ask a few questions. Afterward, I went home that night and researched the possibilities. Could I do a run across North Carolina? How long would it take and would I have to get a helper or, as has been my method on the bike, could I do it myself? Unsupported is a favorite word, meaning that in cycling or running, I wouldn't use that helper. If I did this, I wanted any mistakes made to be mine.

Ed Dupree entered hospice in November just after I had

finished the Outer Banks bike ride. He had lost his ability to talk but I do believe that he understood me when I held his hand and said, "I am going to do the run across North Carolina." Ed's eyes seemed to flicker in recognition. It was up to me to fulfill his dream now.

Ed Dupree died the next day. My planning now had purpose. The Run Across N.C. would happen and getting ready for it took most of the winter. Ed's dream had also become mine.

Come run and walk with me as I cross my home state, a distance of 647 miles. I believe I am only the second person to make this trip unsupported at this writing and the third overall. More than 82,000 miles of lifetime running helped but I was still surprised and challenged time and again over the length of the journey.

Running is my passion, and North Carolina is my favorite state! Please join me on my most physically challenging adventure yet — Murphy to Manteo and more. Let's go explore the Tar Heel state using my feet, my eyes and my pen!

# ED DUPREE

· · · · · · · · · · · · · · · · · · · · · · · · · · · · · · · · · · · · · · ·

E d Dupree was a loving father and husband. He was a talented sportswriter and excellent stat keeper. Ed was dedicated and passionate in all aspects of his life. He was a truly motivating and inspiring coach and always passionate. Ed pursued his goals with record setting fervor. To describe Ed for someone who never had the privilege of meeting him… he was one of a kind.

Ed had a true love of running and fitness and a unique way of setting and achieving goals. These two things set the standard for how he lived each day. When Ed set a goal, he went above and beyond to achieve it. Even when his health was in question, Ed set a goal to run a mile in every county in North Carolina and achieved it. He let nothing stop him from missing a day of running — not rain, not sleet, not snow, not a fever, not the flu, etc. It took the life-ending illness leukemia to snap his running streak. Ed cherished every single moment of his life. He continued his streak of running at least a mile a day for 24 years and 82 days prior to his diagnosis with Acute Myeloid Leukemia.

One goal Ed never was able to achieve was to run across the state of North Carolina. He planned to start in Murphy, N.C., and run to Manteo, N.C., through a meticulously planned route. He had even looked into places to stay along the way. When his health prognosis looked poor, Ed spoke to David Freeze, fellow runner and close friend. Ed wanted David to do the run across North Carolina since Ed no longer would be able to achieve it. He thought that David could do it.

Everyone admired Ed's dedication to life. It should serve as an example for how we should all strive to live ours. Our family is deeply indebted to David Freeze for his accomplishment of running across the state of North Carolina. He was able to achieve a goal that Ed would have been so proud of. We are certain that Ed was with David each step of the way as he trekked across the rural backroads of North Carolina. Ed would have been thrilled to hear the stories of the people David met along the way.

Our family was blessed that Ed Dupree lived for 76 years. When he passed away on Nov. 21, 2017, at the Glenn A. Kiser Hospice House in Salisbury, N.C., we knew our family would never be the same. We will continue to honor his memory through a Memorial 5K Run each May and by awarding a scholarship in his name for a male or female athlete at East Rowan High School each school year.

To close, our family believes everyone who reads this

book about David's journey can learn from one thing Ed used to ask everyone he had once coached — "Are you still running?" Ask yourself this question — it can apply to many facets of your life. Every day, keep running your race and most of all, keep the faith.

*In Memory of Ed Dupree*

*"I have fought the good fight, I have kept the faith, I have finished the race."*
**— 2 Timothy 4:7**

*— By Allison Adams, daughter*

Murphy

Manteo

# CHAPTER 1

*My run across North Carolina — why?*

. . . . . . . . . . . . . . . . . . . . . . . . . . . . . . . . . . . . . . . . . . . . . . . . . . . . . . . . . . . . .

Some days take a different turn than I have planned. In fact, it happens quite often for me. One of these special days stands out in my mind and is really the reason that this journey came about. I had been away on a long bicycle ride from Washington to Wisconsin last summer when I heard that my friend, Ed Dupree, had stopped his daily running streak. Ed had run every day for 24 years and in every county in North Carolina. He had also played on almost all the golf courses in the state with just a few remaining. Some of the courses he missed have since closed.

Ed had lived with a form of blood disease for years and knew that it could eventually get worse. In the meantime, he continued to live life to the fullest. Ed loved sports in general and spent years as a reporter and then sports editor for the Salisbury Post. I have tried hard to remember when I first met Ed but simply can't pin it down. It just seemed that Ed was always around and interested in many of the same things as me. Except for golf! I have tried it a few times and didn't care for the game. It's not enough sweat for me, but I can't say that golf isn't a challenge. It just isn't one on which I cared to spend my time perfecting.

It was an injury that Ed suffered near the end of his years of running that forced him to stop. The leg injury wouldn't heal, forcing him to give up the streak in hopes that he would get better. At about the same time, doctors found that his blood disease had become Acute Myeloid Leukemia, and he was admitted to Novant Health, our local hospital in Salisbury. His daughter, Allison, let me know what had happened and told me that he would be in the hospital locally a few days and would love to have me visit. It was easy for me to go. I couldn't wait to talk with Ed and get the real scoop on what was happening with his health.

When I first saw Ed that September day, he was sitting in his bed reading the paper. Right away, he told me that the doctors had already advised him that he may only have a few months to live and that they were going to try some things to prolong his life. Hearing that, I realized how serious his illness was, but still couldn't imagine not having Ed around. During my visit, he was his usual self, talking sports and running just like we always did.

After we covered the main topics of the day, Ed's demeanor changed, and he began to tell me about one of his few regrets. "I always wanted to run across the state," he said. "Looks like I won't get to do it, but you can. How many miles a day can you do? Could you do 10 miles a day?" I listened quietly, still struggling to grasp the idea that Ed wouldn't be around for many more years. He gave me a rough total distance in miles, saying, "You'll have to get somebody to go along so that person can drop you off and pick you up each day." Ed had planned to get his wife, Bitsy, to do that for him when he first thought of the idea. He had planned to just run and have her pick him up at the end of the day as they worked their way across the state.

I remember asking Ed about possible routes and a few other questions, after which we went on to talk about other interests. When two more of his friends stopped by for a visit, he introduced us, and since I needed to head on to do other things, I left very soon afterwards. I told Ed I would send him a couple of my books that he hadn't yet read and promised to stay in touch.

From the moment I left his room, the idea of running across North Carolina stayed in my mind. I began to wonder if I could in fact do it and started thinking about how it could be done without involving a helper. All of my bike rides so far have been unsupported, and I like that method best. I find it easier to travel alone and make my own decisions. If those made were bad ones, then I was the one who had to live with the consequences. If I was to decide to run across our whole state, I wanted to do it without assistance. I don't remember what else I did that day, but I do remember going home that night and googling "run across NC." I also began to delve into who had done it and any available routes already used. The more I found or didn't find, the more I kept digging.

At least two people had made the trip, one supported and one unsupported. The unsupported one was fairly young, and he had pushed a baby stroller in which to haul his supplies and gear. The other guy wore a light backpack and had help all along the way, with a goal of running it as fast as he could. I read what was available about them and continued to research routes. What kept popping up was that U.S. Highway 64 runs from west of Murphy to on past Manteo, almost all the way to the Atlantic Ocean.

I kept thinking about the solo possibility and considered a backpack as being too unwieldy. I also realized that I might be carrying way too much weight for me to be comfortable. Water needs would push the limits on what I could carry, and I just didn't like that idea. Wearing a backpack on a bike was very hard, and I remembered that my back always tended to get hot, too. Eventually, I began to consider the baby stroller as a possibility and continued researching others. The best time of the year, for me and for the course, had to be spring ... if I could do it at all. There was just so much to consider.

Another adventure was already in the works. I had been researching the possibility of cycling the Outer Banks and had tentatively decided to do it in November. I had in mind to spend about 10 days on a loop north through the Inner Banks and then south on the Outer Banks. Since the available daylight was short, my limited cycling mileage on those days allowed me to have more time than usual at the end of the day for communication, whether directed towards home or otherwise. I heard Ed's name mentioned but didn't see him again for several weeks.

Ed's doctors did have further treatment in mind, and he went off to Wake Forest Baptist Hospital in Winston-Salem to begin it. One report I heard was that he was initially doing well and making progress. Sadly, another later report was that Ed was being moved to hospice. I couldn't believe it! My friend was such a tough and determined guy. Once, Ed needed to get his run in to keep his streak going even though he was terribly sick and didn't want to go outside. He was traveling at the time and staying in a motel room. Ed was so determined that he moved all the furniture to the middle of the room and ran the perimeter until he was sure he had completed a mile.

I arrived home from my bike ride to find that Ed was in fact going to hospice and that the once promising treatment had failed. I talked with my friend, Wayne Crowder — who was also Ed's friend — and we decided to go visit him that next morning. Though Ed had lost his ability to speak, he seemed to be listening intently when someone spoke to him. A few other friends had stopped by the day before, and Bitsy said Ed's spirit had brightened when they talked about running. Although the family was not accepting visitors that day, they were expecting us, and we did get to see him.

My plan was to tell Ed, "Yes, I am going to do the run across North Carolina" in the hopes that he could understand. When the time came for us to say our goodbyes to Ed, I walked over, held his hand and softly stated my commitment to do the run. His eyes seemed to light up, and I hoped he understood me because I was going to make the journey as much for him as for me. My idea was that we could make a good team. On that chilly November day, I set the idea in stone. There would be no backing out.

Ed Dupree died the next day. A few days later, we went to his funeral and heard from his journalistic peers, many athletes that he had coached and plenty of great friends with stories to tell. It was one of the most moving funerals I ever attended. I renewed my commitment to honor him in my own way and vowed to start getting my act together.

I run just about every day, but nobody runs hundreds of miles a month pushing a baby jogger. I didn't own a baby jogger and had never used one. A few runner friends had used them, but had sold theirs or given them away. I went to Walmart and looked at what was there and shopped online, but none of them seemed like the right fit for me. I put the word out that I was looking for one, and a few people offered the economy styles they had purchased at Walmart or Target. Friends kept telling me to find a really good one and to make sure that the front wheel ran straight. Several marathoners with considerable baby jogger experience told me that the front wheel mechanics were the key. One said, "It will drive you crazy if that wheel wobbles and takes you to one side or another and you have to keep correcting it."

While continuing to look for the right stroller, I began assembling my gear. My idea was to use the same tent, sleeping bag, clothes and tools that I had taken on my bike rides. Of course, the running shoes had to be just the right ones. My waterproof bike panniers would ride along and keep the gear together until needed.

Convinced that the simplest route was best, I planned to use much of U.S. Highway 64. I hated those bike rides that had so many turns that it was hard to enjoy the journey. Thinking constantly of when the next turn was coming was never much fun for me. There was an online description of The Mountains to the Sea Trail, but it had dozens of turns. My route needed to be simple, and I wanted to move past that portion of my decision. U.S. 64, or most of it, would be my chosen route.

Still, I saw some parts of the highway that didn't seem necessary. I took a Sunday and drove west to see what the road was like well west of Brevard, all the while making notes of motels and other interesting scenery. Not worried yet about the eastern part of the state, I just wanted to make my way through the mountains and then handle the eastern part as an afterthought. Surely the flat land would be easier anyway.

My schedule had a hole in it that allowed me about four

weeks beginning the last week of March and including the first three weeks of April. This timeframe looked good, and I blocked it on my calendar. The journey began to be real, much more than it had just a few months back when I talked with Ed in his Salisbury hospital bed.

Still without a baby jogger, I decided to move my day of departure to an earlier date. March 3rd seemed right, and my daughter, Amber, committed to take the time to drop me off at the Tennessee line west of Murphy. At that time, she was considering a half marathon in Chattanooga, just 80-plus miles farther west. It might have made more sense to delay the start date, but I wanted to get going. My schedule seemed as good as it was going to get, and my internal excitement was building.

When working on some local racing plans, I contacted Crystal Karriker about what help her organization needed from me and our running club. During the discussion, Crystal mentioned that she had a baby jogger than she didn't need and that it was a good one. She told me that the brand was "Baby Jogger" — which is known for using three actual bicycle wheels and tires unlike the mostly plastic ones from Walmart and other retailers. Crystal told me to come and get it and that she didn't need it back.

First thing the next morning, I stopped by and picked up the baby jogger that had me excited at first sight. The jogger itself was in good shape except for a tire issue and appeared to be very sturdy. I was excited with the gift and immediately contacted Skinny Wheels Bike Shop in Salisbury to see if someone there could take a look at it. Later that day, I stopped in to see Eric and Scott for an assessment of what needed to be done. We decided on a tire replacement and adding a cyclometer to track my mileage and pace. I picked up the jogger the next morning after some additional work on the cyclometer and was essentially ready to go.

After my final choices of clothing and gear were made, I prepared both pannier bags with the items I felt were important enough to push all the way across the state. Another adventure, this one quite special, was going to happen. I couldn't wait!

# CHAPTER 2

### *First day on the road —*
### *Taking the journey one day at a time*

. . . . . . . . . . . . . . . . . . . . . . . . . . . . . . . . . . . . . . . . . . . .

My daughter, Amber, and her fiancé, Jamie, picked me up very early on the morning of Saturday, March 3, to head west. For some reason, I felt more at ease than I often do when a bike ride is getting underway. This probably had to do with me having less worry about the baby jogger than a bike that had just been reassembled and the fact that no plane connections had to be made. It also had to do with the comfort of knowing that I would be remaining in my home state for this whole adventure, a time frame that I expected to take more than 30 days. Being in my home state throughout, of course, meant that help would always be only a few hours away, should the need arise.

Our trip to Murphy and the Tennessee line took close to four hours, and I appreciate Amber and Jamie taking me. My bike rides have always caused me to feel a bit uneasy as the time to kick off the event nears. As we neared Murphy and the Tennessee line, I became quite anxious and was ready to get started. Amber and Jamie had taken a big part of their day to get me where I needed to be. We made it to the Tennessee line just before noon, and I really felt the need to get going because there was still at least 20 miles to cover on my feet by the end of the day.

We stopped at a nearby golf course to use the bathroom and then finally arrived at the state line and began to unload the baby jogger and my bags. I strapped everything into the baby jogger, and we began to make the "start of adventure" photos that we have taken on all my trips. Amber and Jamie scurried around doing just that. Before they left, Jamie made an adjustment on the baby jogger brake, and it worked better afterward. I hugged them both and through a few tears, told them that I had to get going. We had a brief prayer together which supplanted my individual prayers that always start a daily journey. As a side note, I noticed the sign near the state line that stated "560 miles to Manteo," the small town very near the end of my journey. More on that sign later.

With strong legs and plenty of adrenaline, I began pushing and climbed the first hill as Amber and Jamie drove away. My second hill and the first mile of the adventure came soon afterward. I found rumble strips through this particularly hilly section and fought to find road space for the baby jogger. The rumble strip issue would be a big concern for a good portion of my trip to the sea.

Still, it felt good to finally be on the road, this time on

my feet instead of a bike. To be very honest, I had quite a bit of uncertainty about how I would handle the high mileage run/walks each day. The first issue was my concern about where I would spend this first Saturday night. I had called the Sunset Motel the day before and asked about room availability with little success. The motel was totally booked and I had not called anywhere else, planning to work it out once I was on the road. In the early years of these adventures, I always felt much better having arranged for lodging at least 24 hours ahead of my anticipated arrival. That concern had lessened somewhat as evidenced here. I felt confident that something worthwhile would develop.

While battling the rumble strips and oncoming traffic, I experienced the first of my law enforcement encounters. Just less than 10 miles from the start, a sheriff's deputy had pulled over ahead of me and appeared to be waiting. I kept on pushing the stroller until I got to his window, where Deputy Todd Abshier told me that his department had received a call about me. The caller was concerned that I was pushing a baby along the road against traffic. At this point, I did have the canopy up and over the bags strapped into the stroller. My sign stating "Murphy to Manteo, Run Across NC" made the first portion of our conversation easier. I remembered seeing two Hispanic ladies who slowed down, and one of them pointed at me. I had just waved and kept going and looking back on it, wondered if they were the ones who had called. Clearly, there was no room for a baby

13

between the bags but this would certainly not be the last such encounter.

I enjoyed talking with Deputy Abshier, who told me about his upcoming trip out west for vacation. He was a friendly guy and a good conversationalist who was just doing his job. I saw Deputy Abshier later as he passed by on the road again, and we both waved. I decided that pulling the canopy back was the best thing to do. My bags were red with safety triangles and quite easy to see.

Deputy Abshier also gave me some advice on lodging in the Murphy area and one specific place that he suggested I avoid. I planned to follow his advice and find something better once I got to town. Just four minutes after I got back on the road, I received a call from Ashley Canning with the Sunset Motel. Ashley had answered my inquiry the night before and told me that she was sold out for Saturday evening. I had asked her to call if anything changed and darned if she didn't do just that. One of her reservations had cancelled at the last minute, and Ashley said she wanted to give me first shot at that room, since it was smaller and would be just perfect for me and a baby jogger.

So I now had a room for my first night on the road and nice weather that was starting to turn a little bit nippy as the afternoon wore on. One of those sign poles with all the mileages to towns and cities across the region came along next, and Manteo just seemed very far away. But "one day at a time" was my mantra for this trip and each day was sure to include something memorable. What I knew right now though was that I still had to reach Murphy.

I ran/walked into town and stopped at a convenience store to fill up on several snacks and more water. My phone directions were fairly clear on getting to the motel through the old part of town but I took time to confirm them with the extremely friendly store clerk. He and a customer both asked about my journey, and I began the first discussion I had that day other than the one with Deputy Abshier. My bags still had some room for food from a McDonald's located just across the road, and I took time to stop and buy some. No more stops would be required once I found the Sunset Motel. My feet were ready to leave the road, but they couldn't quite yet.

The Sunset Motel was just what I had hoped for. Though it was an older style motel, it had been remodeled nicely and was located in a quiet area. I found a very pleasant Ashley expecting me and enjoyed yet another conversation with her. She told me that her parents owned the motel and shared some of its history and how they had bought and remodeled what had started out as a very seedy building. She said her family didn't buy the other part of the motel which still stood vacant across the road.

After registering, I checked into my bright and stylish room. Just outside the door was a replica of the 10 Commandments, and the last thing I did outside on that day was to take a picture of them. Inside, I found a breakfast basket already in place all the while knowing that most of that food wouldn't last the evening. My hunger meter was by now registering very high. The food already purchased really hit the spot as I typed away chronicling my day's activities. It felt great to be in the room, almost fed and warm against the ever-dropping temperature outside after 22 mostly afternoon miles.

With my daily story submitted to the paper and most of the first round of food stowed away, my next goal for the evening was to take a hot shower. I have been known to linger in a hot shower on days that challenged me and also use that time for my evening prayers. While some might say that these things should be done separately, I am sure that God understands because I am never in a hurry to finish my shower or prayers. After watching a small amount of TV and answering some emails, my first day walking across North Carolina was close to being history. Before calling it a day, I stopped by the office to thank Ashley one more time for following through after her cancellation.

Anxious as always to get on the road, I got out of bed at 6 a.m. when the sky was still very dark. I almost never sleep that late but there was no rush to start the day until there was enough daylight to see and be seen. The temperature was 26 degrees, and nearly all of my available clothes would be needed to start the day. Ashley had told me the evening before how to find Walmart and still be on my way to reconnect with U.S. 64. I was back on the road by daylight when I crossed the Valley River quickly and seemed to be heading out of town. I saw a man beside the river and decided to ask if I was going the right way to Walmart and 64. Apparently I scared him because he quickly hopped in his car and tried to exit around the entrance of the little park to avoid me. I never got close enough to ask for directions before he drove away. It seems that people are not quite sure what to think of a guy operating a baby jogger on a very cold morning. All my clothes plus a hooded raincoat did make for toasty conditions.

With no one else to ask and not making much sense of my phone directions, I turned around and headed back through the downtown in the same general direction from which I had come. Not much traffic was on the road this Sunday morning, but I did see a sign more directly toward U.S. 64 and followed it.

Murphy has a vibrant and historic downtown that highlights both the Hiawassee and Valley rivers as area attractions. Before the 1838 beginning of the Cherokee Indian journey to Oklahoma — later known as the Trail of Tears — many of the Indians were gathered against their will into Murphy's Fort Butler. More than 4,000 Cherokees died on that relocation journey to their new home.

I wanted to get to Walmart and see if I could find a small radio to help pass the time. I also needed to see if I could get a new battery for my cyclometer, a distance-measuring device. For the second straight trip, my cyclometer wouldn't work correctly. The brand new one on the stroller was lighting up but not registering so I hoped a new battery would get it going. Ashley had told me where to find Walmart but I was unsure of her route and went a mile off course in search of the store. Just to make sure I was headed the right way, I stopped at a convenience store with no customers and little product on the shelves, but being run by a clerk with plenty of advice on how to proceed for the rest of the day. I followed none of his advice, which included backtracking through town to avoid traffic. The clerk did tell me that Walmart was just over the next hill.

The last small AM-FM radio on the rack was calling my name, and with batteries in hand, I immediately put the earbuds in and started walking toward my rendezvous with U.S. 64 and a journey toward Hayesville. The radio, made by Motorola, was of good quality and did well at picking up the Sunday morning hymns played so prominently in the area. I found a great station and immediately quickened my pace while singing some of my favorites. Singing loudly, I should add.

The bright sun helped usher in slightly warmer temperatures and another gentle tailwind as I rejoined U.S. 64. By now, my very sore quadriceps began to loosen up some, and I was able to take off my windbreaker/raincoat. One clear thought came to my mind about running and/or walking as opposed to cycling on these adventures. Cycling seems almost supersonic as compared to the pace that I was able to make on my feet while pushing the baby jogger. The one mile out of the way to Walmart while dodging traffic and rumble strips, those indentions in the pavement to wake sleepy drivers, and the return trip seemed to take forever.

The brilliant day and my hymn singing continued as I headed toward Hayesville. I met Mike Keifer, who was cycling to Murphy to play tennis with his sister. Mike had done some long-distance cycling and had even been to Duluth, Minnesota, which was the largest city on my latest long-distance bike journey this past summer. I pedaled from Washington through Wisconsin and enjoyed Duluth and Lake Superior on another picture-perfect day. As is my custom, I asked Mike for a picture that could show up in the Salisbury Post. His demeanor changed quite a bit and he said, "I don't want to take a picture. I have seen it in the post office, and I don't make good pictures." We started to part and then talked some more before I asked again. Still no pictures. We ended up going our separate ways that time.

I pushed on toward Hayesville, immensely enjoying my radio, the nice day and my own singing. No one else has ever enjoyed my singing and likely never would. On one particularly quiet stretch, I saw a small monument to the Cherokee and the Valley Towns Mission. On this monument, I read that the Cherokee children were being educated in the nearby mission until right before the Trail of Tears, which was recorded as happening in 1836. I am not sure of the reason for the different years, but Wikipedia does say that the relocation went on for several years. However, 1838 seems to be the most prominent year in most historical accounts.

The next interesting thing I noticed was an older model small plane that circled above me several times. I kept waving, and finally he peeled off to head south. There was lots of various roadkill in the mountains, most of it possums now no longer able to climb trees.

Hayesville had the first real grocery store I had encountered on my journey, and I took time to stop in. It is always great to find a real grocery store on the route when I am biking, and this time it was even more special to find one while on foot. I already knew that no side trips to find a grocery were likely so this one had me excited. I got some fruit, a good buy on cookies and several yogurts but needed someone to scan their Ingle's card at the self-scanner so I could take advantage of the advertised prices, and right on cue, a nice man walked over to do it. I was out within five minutes and back on the road.

Mike Kiefer had told me about two places to stay along my route, and I was ready find one. The Deerfield Inn overlooks Lake Chatuge, and I kept trying to reach someone there on the phone. No one answered, and no one called back. I saw it as I passed and some cars were parked there, and a man appeared to be walking into the office. The view would have been great had it been open, but I just kept going. Just a short mile or so down the road, I found Kiefer's recommended place, the Chatuge Mountain Inn. I had called there earlier and the manager told me that she had a room for me but would be gone for a family event. If I wanted the room, she offered to leave me a key and the room number hanging on the office door. She also told me to make sure that I brought food as there weren't any stores located close by.

By now very sore and tired after 21 miles, which still seemed like a long way to me, I found the Chatuge Mountain Inn and my envelope on the door. My room was very nice and in a quiet location. I settled in just ahead of another chilly night to write my story for the day and reload what appeared to be a bottomless pit of hunger. My goal of getting some extra rest was met, too, just after I settled the bill. The very large room for me and the baby jogger, a hot shower and peaceful surroundings were just what I needed for the night. My legs were taking a beating, and tomorrow would be a longer day.

At this point, I realized how important it was to have a top quality baby jogger for my long journey. The possibility that I could have started all of this with one of those plastic wheel joggers from Walmart or Target now seemed like old news but it nearly happened. Crystal Karriker provided me with the perfect gift for the trip with her baby jogger. Though well worn, it still had plenty of miles of use left in it. Currently it was carrying about 35 pounds of gear and supplies. The front tire ran true every mile, just as it should.

I don't believe the plastic ones would have worked.

I slept very well that night and awoke to another chilly morning. With a long day on tap and a good but lightly traveled U.S. 64 in front of my motel, I had already planned on a very early start. My cyclometer battery purchase had only marginally affected the performance of the cyclometer. It still wasn't operating correctly, but I knew that Hayesville was just 34 miles from the motel front door, according to the manager, and the road looked to be in pretty good shape. My trip on this day would be further than I had ever made it in a day and would include some climbing. The longest day of running in my life was 32 miles about 30 years ago, a breakfast run from my farm to Statesville. My legs were even more sore this morning, and no improvement was expected anytime soon. Some good motel choices seemed to be available in Franklin, but I didn't have one selected.

Another important word had just been mentioned on the radio. "Snow" and cold rain were unexpectedly in the forecast, much different from the 10 days of predicted good weather when I first started. Once again, I planned to take "just one day at a time" with the goal of making the most of the longest day so far.

With just a hint of daylight visible, I left the warm room and headed east, my direction of choice for the foreseeable future. My flashing red lights on the sides of the baby jogger alerted traffic and gave me room as did the wide road, although some of it included the dreaded rumble strips. I spotted a few coins on the shoulders of the road that morning and stopped to pick them up. Collecting found money has long been a running habit, and it would continue with this journey to the Atlantic.

With the temperature at about 33 degrees, I felt really comfortable wearing plenty of clothes. Walking/running as opposed to cycling are really quite different when it comes to body comfort. The body builds up a lot of heat when running or walking fast, way more than it does on a cold bike. I was careful not to get too sweaty because the sweat would get colder if I didn't generate it continuously. The sun began to rise and was quite beautiful, but I couldn't get a good photo due to the giant trees and uphill climb.

The rumble strips continued as I met little traffic while entering the Nantahala National Park. The road was newly paved, my favorite kind, and I made good time while climbing up to the Winding Stairs Gap at 3,820 feet. Often during the climb, I thought about how nice this area would be for a bike ride. The climb was on a good road with little traffic, and the grade was not torturous. Some of the scenery was spectacular and was at its best near the top on the initial decline.

Thinking that I was making good time, I stopped on several occasions to start shopping for motels. I wanted to find one with a good rate since I paid too much for the one on the second night and maybe the first night as well. It has been a game that I play, trying to find the right motel for the best price, knowing that I will only spend a very few waking hours there and be sleeping the rest of the time before leaving early the next morning. But as I found out later that day, going out of the way on foot for a better price is not as much fun as on a bike when I can cover the distance much quicker. I contacted the Sapphire Motel near Franklin's hospital and thought I had found a good match.

Pushing the jogger on along 64 went well for most of the day until I neared Franklin. That portion of the highway had a wide shoulder, no rumble strips and no real concerns until I got to town. When I asked Siri on my iPhone, she seemed really confused about the best route to the Sapphire Motel, so I called ahead and asked the person who answered. I hate to say it but when you get a desk clerk who doesn't speak English, trouble looms. She said that I just needed to look for McDonald's and that the motel was behind it near the Hardee's. I asked, "Will I be able to see this area from US 64?" "Oh yes," was her reply.

It was starting to get late and much cooler and I was making a good pace when I realized that I was passing out of town on the eastern side. I had seen no McDonald's or Hardee's and called the lady back. She gave me the same reply, "Look for the both of them and we are right behind them." So, I continued on. When another exit loomed ahead, I decided to take it, stopping to ask a guy at a phone store for directions. He told me that I had missed the McDonald's, but that he didn't know anything about a Hardee's or the Sapphire Motel. I backtracked along 64 with traffic building all the time during rush hour. I kept checking my phone and got mixed information.

Finally, when totally confounded, I checked Google Assistant, which cleared it all up. I was on U.S. 64, which became U.S. 64 Truck. The motel was not on U.S. 64 Truck but was near Highlands Road, which I found out much later was U.S. 64 regular but only south of town. All of this was very confusing to me. With this early info, I just decided to follow Google Assistant's directions and go to the motel, at which I finally arrived after dark. McDonald's and Hardee's were both there, and so was the hospital. The motel was cheap for good reason, but it didn't matter. I was 40 miles into a journey that realistically had included between four and five miles of being lost or misdirected. I was very frustrated but finally in the dry should the impending cold rain start. Not a single decent conversation had occurred on this day with my focus solely on completing the journey and finding shelter.

I was finally able to sit down in the room after buying some food. It was late, nearly 8:30 p.m., after having found my way to the motel in the dark. It was time to relax a little bit and send my story to the Post before planning for tomorrow and hoping to get a handle on the different U.S. 64s. It turned out that I was premature in that thought because as I began to work, I needed to charge my iPad. I couldn't find the cables anywhere and realized that I had left them at the Chatuge Mountain Inn. There was nothing to do but find more, and I immediately thought of a Hot Spot convenience store that I had passed on the way in. With tired legs and a bit of exasperation at my dumb move of leaving them behind, I headed back out of the room to find replacements. The Hot Spot had them, and the clerk was really pleased to sell them to me at a price that I considered way too high. These were the knockoffs and looked OK except for the price. The store also had some made by Apple, but two of them would have cost more than my motel room. I kicked myself again, bought the knockoffs and headed back to the motel. Both worked fine, and my long and frustrating day finally came to an end. But the frustration would not end when my head hit the pillow.

Passing through the downtown area in the dark let me get at least some idea of what Franklin was like. It is known as a trail town because the Appalachian Trail passes nearby. I had seen an AT crossing near the Winding Stair Gap, which is famous for its gems and minerals. The locals call Franklin the "Gem Capital of the World." The town has about 4,000 residents.

Usually I sleep quite well on my various adventures. The Sapphire Motel was quiet although it seemed to be jampacked. On this night, I awakened thinking of the pending rain and that I might still be lost. When I looked out the door, I saw that only light rain was falling and decided that it did not appear heavy enough to delay my departure. I got ready, checked with my phone and map directions until ready to head out the door. Siri showed that U.S. 64 was right up the road, but I had to start out on Highlands Avenue to get there. Surely this wouldn't be as hard as it was last evening.

With the rain slowly intensifying into a steady downpour, I ended up delaying my departure based on the forecast of the rain lessening as the morning passed. I waited an hour and dozed briefly, but when the weather didn't improve, I walked out the door and said goodbye to the Sapphire Motel. I turned onto Highlands Avenue and headed east. Now under a steady rain, I saw the sign that pointed toward U.S. 64 and followed it. After about two miles, I realized that I was yet again on U.S. 64 Truck, which was not the right road. I stopped at a motel and asked for some clarity on what was happening. The desk clerk told me that if I wanted to go to Highlands, I had to get back on regular 64 and that I would reach it about two more miles down the road. That seemed confusing, but I thought it would be OK since I had a clear direction. Siri was oblivious to any of this. I covered the two miles as the rain continued to fall until it was a hard downpour, and I saw the Sapphire Motel again. I had managed to make a four-mile loop and had ended right back where I started. This couldn't be right, so I stopped at a busy convenience store and asked again. A very nice clerk took time to explain what had happened. She said, "Take Highlands Avenue and stay on it way past the turnoff for

U.S. 64, the truck version. Once you are leaving town, you will see that Highlands Avenue becomes U.S. 64 and it will take you right into Highlands." I bought some snacks and got some plastic shopping bags to cover my mittens even though they were already wet and cold. I finally knew what to do.

After losing my charging cables and becoming lost since I got to Franklin, I figured my luck had to improve. I forgot to mention yet another issue of the morning. I got an early call from an unknown number, and I didn't answer it. After checking the message, I was told that my debit card had been hacked and used twice already in Kenya and that the bank had voided it. My debit card no longer existed. I wondered if I could make it out of Franklin with no more issues.

There was plenty on my mind as I did finally leave Franklin and found the right U.S. 64. The road began to climb and had several severe switchbacks with no road shoulder. After the delayed start and getting lost, I needed to get going, but there was no way to run with the baby jogger. The drivers would fly around those switchbacks and then slam on their brakes when they saw me hugging the side of the road. Deciding that there had to be a better way, I crossed to the other side and found the going much easier. The uphill traffic was going slower and had a better sightline of my bright yellow raincoat. I felt much safer.

This portion of the journey was extremely beautiful, but in retrospect, the most challenging area had yet to be experienced. I was in the Cullasaja Gorge, and the beautiful river was rushing downhill as my jogger kept going uphill. Both Dry Falls and Bridal Veil Falls were right on U.S. 64 and quite spectacular. Dry Falls appeared to be aptly named because visitors can walk behind it and stay dry. It was cloudy, foggy and chilly, and I realized that Highlands might have to be my final destination for the day. I finally reached there about 5 p.m. after a nearly all-day rain, several calls about the debit card and getting lost that morning.

I checked for available motels in Highlands and found nothing affordable. In fact, the ones online were incredibly expensive. I saw a small covered bridge as I entered town and stopped to take some photos just as Davis Moore came running by. Davis ran toward me and asked about my journey. He wanted to know if I had climbed all the way up the gorge that day. Of course, I had, but I should have made it farther after a whole day of walking. Davis confirmed that there were no cheap motels and said he didn't know of any that were affordable enough for my budget. I pressed on.

Now totally sure that I could not make it to Cashiers before dark, I had to call ahead and release a room there before it was too late. After finally getting my story submitted back in Franklin, I had left a message at a motel in Cashiers inquiring about a room for tonight and got a pleasant call back with a half-price rate because of my journey.

Faced with having to find a place in Highlands, I went to work on it. I asked a guy who worked for Ace Hardware and his answer was, "I couldn't afford to stay in any of the places here." Two ladies were walking up the sidewalk, and I asked them. Both said they lived in Highlands and totally understood my dilemma. One of them recommended the Mitchell Lodge and Cottages. I looked up Mitchell Lodge on my phone and saw some high but more affordable rates than the other places. I called there and left my information with the answering service. It had to work out so I started walking that way as darkness began to close in.

So far, I had passed through Cherokee and Clay counties, sure that snow was coming and I was getting colder by the minute. Winter wasn't done yet.

# CHAPTER 3

*Snow and more mountains*
*but walking toward the sunshine*

. . . . . . . . . . . . . . . . . . . . . . . . . . . . . . . . . . . . . . . . . . . . . . . . . .

Beaten back a little bit by the day's events preceding my arrival in Highlands, I hoped that things would work out for me to get a room at the Mitchell Lodge and Cottages. I didn't get a call back from the lodge though the message on the answering service assured me that someone would return my call. I kept walking, optimistic that the large lodge would have a room for me. Just past a grocery store, I found the lodge next door. It was a beautiful place and I saw the office lights on even though there were no cars in sight. Some of the motels in the area were not open in what they considered offseason, and my hope was that this large one was.

I walked into the office and probably looked like a drenched and cold wreck, which in fact was pretty close to being true. I met a bright-eyed female clerk who seemed quite harried. She asked if she could help me, and I told her I needed a room for the night and had seen some prices online. Her first comments were, "Oh, those prices are for pre-bookings. You have to pay for them weeks early." I thought to myself, "OK, I need to just cut to the chase and find out how much I would have to pay to get a room." It was getting dark, snow was predicted within a few hours, and for the first time, I admitted to myself that I was tired.

The clerk told me that I could get a room and quoted me a higher-than-hoped-for price. I had no real options but was able to talk her down a little bit. When she found out that I was from Salisbury, she seemed more interested and told me that Lee Street was named for someone in her family. The bottom line was that I took a room at her price and thanked her, ready to get off my feet and out of the cold.

I opened the room and was absolutely amazed by what I found. The room had a lodge feeling and was huge, complete with a fireplace and balcony with rocking chairs overlooking a creek. It offered all the best of everything, including a small kitchen. The brightly wooded room seemed a reasonable reward for a very challenging day. I walked back uphill to the highest priced grocery that I have ever seen and quickly grabbed an overpriced sub sandwich and some other snacks to recharge my energy. I was ready to enjoy the room and its fireplace after 24 miles and climbing to an elevation of 4,318 feet.

I submitted my story, took a long, hot shower and began to eat everything in sight. I know that the staff members who follow me into these rooms must think that at least three or four people have spent the night based on all the food wrappers and trash. Usually, I finally just get tired of eating and stop even though still hungry.

Another thing about the motel rooms in which I stay on these adventures is my hope to leave them as clean as I found them. Most people probably don't take the time to straighten up the rooms nor do they put all their trash in grocery or store bags instead of the trashcans. It just seems right to me, and I imagine the surprise on their faces when they do see the room. Just so you know, I am not that neat at home.

After a wonderful night's sleep and the knowledge that the first 100 miles of my journey were in the rearview mirror, I was excited to get rolling the next morning even though it was snowing and a light blanket of white had already covered the grassy areas. The highest elevations above 3,500 feet were supposed to get snow, and since I was well above that, at least that portion of the forecast had come true. The earlier temperature of 30 degrees dropped to 26 as the snow intensified. Between 7 and 9 a.m., the snow had begun to fall quite heavily, and the traction with my shoes began to suffer. For the first time ever on one of my journeys, I didn't know if my feet and running shoes could do the job. The roads were very slick and to make matters worse, the road narrowed and had no shoulder at all just east of Highlands. Three wonderful people stopped to offer rides and to check on me. Nobody mentioned a baby. A fourth person stopped to tell me that I had better get out of the road and onto the sidewalks. I had encountered the first jerk of the trip, who managed to hold up traffic as he yelled at me. I told him, "Just go on. I am not listening." A lot more was said, but nothing useful. Regardless, there were no sidewalks. My response wasn't the best, but nobody like that will control what I do, and it wasn't at all difficult to put the conversation behind me.

U.S. 64 had no regular shoulders in this area so I often crossed back and forth to find the best place to walk. There was no opportunity to run, and the slippery footing made me sometimes have to fight for traction. Late in the morning, the snow stopped and glimpses of sun popped through as the temperature moderated. The 11 miles from Highlands to Cashiers went by quicker than I had expected with these conditions.

Just before entering Cashiers, I was pulled over by Blake Watson, a sergeant with the Jackson County Sheriff's Department. Someone had reported a homeless person pushing a shopping cart down the highway, and again, nothing was said about a baby. The plastic bags on my hands might have contributed to my appearance of being homeless. I enjoyed meeting Sergeant Watson, and we talked about various things. Upon leaving, he wished me luck, and told me to call him if I had any trouble later in the day. Before he left, we made a couple of selfie photos, something that I don't usually do, but it seemed appropriate.

I forgot to mention the two teenage girls who stopped

me on the way to Highlands the previous day to ask, "Are you really running across the state? We think that is the coolest thing!" I told them I was running as much as I could but had walked nearly all of that day.

After entering Cashiers, I stopped to get two egg and cheese biscuits at the booming BP convenience store. I didn't stay long but still wished I had made better time the previous day to reach the motel connection nearby. There was nothing to do but push on toward Sapphire against some very heavy traffic with no road shoulders. I remember spending quite a bit of time off the road while trucks and other vehicles passed by, then jumping back on the road for the easier pushing as long as I could.

Somewhere near here, I realized that my cyclometer had again quit working even though there was a display on the screen. The mileage was not tabulating, and the pace didn't show either. I looked closer and the little metal magnet-sending unit on the spoke was gone. I needed to find a bike shop, and those would be few and far between on this trip. In the meantime, I was back to using road sign mileages and mile markers if they existed.

Back on the road toward Sapphire, I totaled 22 miles by the time I reached the Brook Trout Inn. This was the only motel nearby and turned out to be quite nice. I had called the day before and got an adjusted price. I talked to the owner and told him that I was at the motel and he replied, "Make yourself at home in the lobby and I will be there within a half hour. I am just getting off work." A new Dollar General had just been built next door, and I stopped in to do some dinner shopping but found little that caught my eye. I called a BP convenience store down the road that the clerk said was just a mile away.

While waiting in the lobby of the inn, I went ahead and typed my story for the day and submitted it with my photos. It felt great to have this out of the way before dark. I met Anne Braman, who was also staying at the motel, as I worked, and we talked a little. She and her husband, Bill, were visiting the area from Traverse City, Michigan, and just that same day had committed to buying a house close by. The inn owner still had not arrived, and Ann left. A short time later, Bill Braham walked in. He asked about my trip and was a heck of a nice guy. We had talked for a few minutes when he offered to take me to the BP store and get something to eat. It turned out that the mile that it took to get to the store, according to the clerk, was more than two, and I was relieved to not have to walk the four miles. I looked around the store to pick out some things and before I knew it, Bill was paying for everything.

Bill and I talked a little more upon our return to the Brook Trout Inn, and I took his picture. He and Ann definitely will get a copy of this book when it is completed. In the meantime, the owner had arrived and had my room heater going. Another cold day had passed, and I had dropped 1,000 feet in elevation, lessening the chance for more predicted snow the next day. It was still likely to be very cold when I left the next morning. Bitter cold winds with temperatures in the low 20s were forecast. I settled into my room still a little earlier than usual and enjoyed more time off my feet. I had a shin splint and some tenderness in my right foot. Both sets of my toes hurt but at least one change had happened that might alleviate some of these issues.

I actually started out planning to alternate between two pairs of running shoes, the Altra Paradigms and the New Balance 880s. I did that for the first couple of days, and my feet hurt so bad after 10 or more miles in the 880s that I changed to the Altras fulltime. I am not sure why this happened but I do know that it worked. At home, I use the 880s as my top shoes and rotate them with the Altras. My feet never hurt, but it probably had more to with the change in form from pushing the baby jogger and being on them for so much more time. At least my legs were less sore by this time.

One funny thing that happened on this day involved haste and deception. When running or walking, I seem to need to pee much more often than when on a bike. I have tried to hydrate more effectively, after the blood clot issues of the past, which has resulted in additional roadside stops. The need gets quite strong sometimes, and I have to hustle to find a place where I will not be seen. I was not too far into the woods and trying to make good turnaround time. Going out too quickly caused me to miss a root or vine that snagged my shoe, and I fell hard in a shuddering, face to the ground crash. Just as in the past, I hopped up and made like nothing had happened before heading back to the stroller.

My night at the Brook Trout Inn was very relaxing and comfortable with an excellent heating system. I dreaded the forecasted wind and cold of the next morning as I hit the bed, but found conditions less frigid upon arising. The wind was moderate and the temperatures less chilling than expected at 26 degrees. And there was no snow! The owner of the inn had provided supplies to "make your own breakfast," but I didn't wait around to use them.

As the sun rose over the mountains and trees, I found out quite quickly that the sunny spots were the most comfortable. I also found unusual traffic conditions that confused me quite a bit. With no road shoulders and a quick rough descent into a ditch, I didn't make good time while off the road. My real problem came with the frequency of traffic. No cars or trucks would meet me for five minutes at a time, and then a mad bumper-to-bumper rush would provide an onslaught for several minutes. Over and over this happened, often pushing me off the road, and I became more curious each time.

The source of all the traffic surprises was a massive road project that I later learned included straightening U.S. 64 through the area. Several layers of flagmen were holding up traffic while large equipment moved back and forth on the roads. Once released, the drivers rushed to make up lost time, and the convoy speed probably increased because of it.

Another almost law enforcement stop happened shortly afterward. I neared Lake Toxaway and noticed several nice collections of homes in the area. A security vehicle drove to the edge of the road at one of the gates and waited for me to get near his car. Security guard Mike West got out of his car and walked out to wait for me at the road, telling me that his office had been told that I was walking a baby carriage down the busy road and that both the baby and me must be really cold. I flipped back the top canopy and showed West that it was my bags — and not a baby — in the carriage. My explanation and sign on the stroller seemed to convince him and I was free to go, which he communicated to someone he called the dispatcher.

Several large dump trucks had been passing me over the last several days, and I soon realized where they were going. The dirt-moving equipment in the construction area was being used to remove a huge hill. Truck after truck was being loaded with dirt and sent away while another pulled into line. I definitely walked through this area as it was hilly and congested, while many of the equipment operators and flagmen waved or said hello.

The last flagman was Sadiq Harris, and he motioned me over to talk. He had a bright smile and asked what I was doing, possibly as a break from the monotonous work and cold temperatures. He questioned why anybody would journey across the state on foot and how I stayed in such good shape. Sadiq was a fun guy, and I enjoyed the short break.

After leaving the construction area and passing through Rosman, consisting of a trading post and a gem mine, I received two great gifts. The road shoulders grew wide, and snow flurries started to fall. Those flurries only lasted for about 10 minutes, and during that time, the wind started to blow at 15 to 25 mph as a tailwind.

I was surprised to find a historical marker listing a NASA tracking station that functioned from 1982 to 1995. My next surprise was finding yet another Dollar General and a convenience store right beside the road, but down a big hill unless I went to the next exit and followed the road like normal people would. Seldom described as being normal, I took the shorter and much steeper route but still survived along with my trusty baby jogger. I needed new batteries for my radio after discovering that this model only provided major static on low battery no matter how strong the station was. Inside the store, I had to round out the purchase monetarily and chose to do it with Reese's Cups, my personal peanut butter and chocolate energy fuel.

A humorous lesson was learned in front of this store after I powered up the radio. It was cold enough for me to have worn my long running pants and the drawstring was frayed, so much so that I expected it to break at any time. For some reason, I had tied the drawstring way too tight and couldn't get it untied. One lady went in the store and came back out as I worked on the drawstring and gave me an odd look the second time. Homeless, with a baby, and unable to get out of my long pants are big dilemmas. But with my usual determination and after eating the Reese's snack, I got the drawstring untied and packed away my long pants. With shorts, a tailwind, good music and loaded with confidence, I headed east again on U.S. 64 while "Walking in the Sunshine!" That big bright globe had just reappeared.

I was walking at the time and saw a black pickup truck pull over way ahead of me at the next turnoff. Daniel and Dee Nunnaley had stopped to talk and ask a few questions. Daniel had seen me earlier that morning and now became the third person of the day to see if I needed or wanted a ride. He and Dee live in Cashiers and were on their way to Morganton. I told them that I was also headed there but had to do it on my own two feet.

Finally, after 21 miles in for the day, I arrived in Brevard and could see in the distance a motel that I couldn't wait to visit. U.S. 64 made a sharp left turn just inside Brevard and located right at that intersection was the very cool and historic Sunset Motel, looking very much like a Route 66 makeover, complete with a neon sign. I was just several hundred yards away. The first order of business was to stop at a newly refurbished and huge convenience store for food. After seeing the good prices, especially on pizza, I decided to get some things and order a pizza later.

The owner of the Sunset Motel had given me a great rate because of my adventure so I pushed the jogger across the street and met Elizabeth, the manager, in the office. Elizabeth knew Emily Ford, a friend from home, and also offered to help me with finding a bike shop for the ailing cyclometer. She took time to call a couple of places, where their new ones were way high, and one place that didn't have any in stock. The last place was about four miles away, and I didn't want to do that eight-mile round trip for the rest of the day. I would try again tomorrow, a Friday.

Elizabeth's office was decorated with lots of old signs and plenty of Route 66 memorabilia. I grabbed a couple of tourist pamphlets and went on to my room. The distance of 21 miles seemed fairly easy on this day, but I was still hungry. I ordered pizza for the first and only time on this trip. Maybe eating a whole pizza would make me feel stuffed for at least a few minutes, but probably not. Another awesome night passed, during which I took some great pictures of the neon sign. This one had all the lights working, unlike most of those remaining on Route 66.

Waking up very early the next morning and preparing to head for Hendersonville, I faced the coldest morning yet. The soreness in my legs continued to lessen, and I felt stronger, possibly starting to find a groove. No doubt, this was an interesting journey, but there was a long way to go with plenty more hills and mountains. Forecasts had begun to include more snow and rain in the next few days. The worst predictions called for several days of wet and cold.

Friday morning started off well, and the cold came in

with a calm wind, pleasant in its uniqueness so far. My mittens were good but they were not going to keep my hands warm this morning as the temperature dipped to 19 degrees. My Hot Hands packets were all gone, but I had some vinyl gloves and had heard hands wouldn't get cold in them. That statement turned out to be fanciful and false. I had the mittens on over the vinyl gloves, and my hands kept getting progressively colder. Finally, after the greenway that I had been using to stay out of traffic left U.S. 64, I stopped at a convenience store to warm up a little and see about getting some more Hot Hands. None were available but the sun was rising so fast that I decided to dispose of the vinyl gloves and try using just the mittens. That worked for the time being, probably because the vinyl gloves generated sweat and that sweat got cold. I would look for the Hot Hands on down the road.

After passing Etowah and entering Horseshoe, I found a small hardware store on the left side of the road. Thinking that this might be the right place to find some Hot Hands, I went inside to see. The first person I met was a jovial guy named David Ward, who was seated at the counter. I told him about my journey, and David told me that he was president of the motorcycle ministry for Western North Carolina. Ward offered some good information, but I was unsure of what he meant while we were talking. He said, "This is a terrible road ahead!" I wondered because the road outside had wide shoulders and had been great since leaving

43

Brevard. Not wanting to ask and knowing that I couldn't change the road ahead, I asked him about bike shops. He told me about one ahead on my route to Hendersonville, but it sounded complicated to try to find. Hopefully Siri or more likely Google Assistant would help me.

The clerk or possibly the owner sold me some Hot Hands. They were $1 apiece, and I didn't think a thing of it at the time. I bought four packets and thanked the clerk, and especially David, who seemed genuinely interested in my trip.

Heading out of Horseshoe, it became immediately apparent that I was in for a challenge. The road was narrow, with no shoulders at all, and there was plenty of traffic. In fact, this was the hardest sustained section of road for me and the baby jogger. The ditch began at the white line, which left me pushing the baby jogger at an odd angle most of the time. I felt lucky to be able to keep just the back right wheel on the pavement, which stabilized the bouncing more than if all the wheels were in the grass. For six miles, I spent more time off the road than on it. Heading into Hendersonville, the traffic got even heavier with what I envisioned were workers getting off early on a Friday afternoon.

I found the bike shop that David Ward had mentioned as I got into town. It was just a couple of blocks off U.S. 64, and I rolled the baby jogger right through the front door. Michael Robinson, the owner of the Bicycle Company, listened quietly to my reason for bringing the jogger to him and immediately responded, "Well, it might be that all you need is the weighted sensor. The unit itself looks OK, and if it will read the sensor, then you should be in business. Most of the sensors are about the same." My joy at getting this important item working again was probably a little hard to understand for others, but on any trip, it is important for me to know where I am. Nothing is better on the cycling adventures than an accurate cyclometer, and now I needed it even more on the slower pace that my feet provided.

Once we were sure that the cyclometer was working again, I asked Michael how much I owed him. He would only take a $1 for the diagnosis, fitting it and the part itself. How could I complain? I promised to send him a book as soon as I could get it finished, but since he knows bicycles, I will send him a couple of my previous books, too.

It was while walking just down the street ready to join U.S. 64 again that I met DeDe Walton and Ginger Fisher, who were also on the sidewalk. They asked about my journey, and we had a very pleasant conversation. Ward, Robinson, Walton and Fisher made my day and just as I have always said, the journey proves to be about the people I meet along the way.

Only a short two miles away on more good road shoulders was a small Day's Inn that offered a low price online the night before, and I had taken it. I didn't realize at the time that I was going to be charged an online booking fee. This showed up when I checked into the motel and discovered that the good price was not quite the deal that I had thought it was. On the way to the motel, I found three more dimes and netted a total of $0.55 for the day. Ed Dupree's daughter, Allison, told me that her dad enjoyed doing this, too, and that he just might be leaving those coins ahead as a reward. She texted me, saying that he would have loved this trip, and I totally agreed. I think of him often and felt like he was right there with me all along.

At check in, I apparently met the owner, who was ecstatic that I was staying in his motel. He asked quite a few questions and offered to help me with directions. Not too concerned at this point, I still let him print out some Mapquest routes. For some reason, when printed for walking or running, those maps take you off onto sideroads and a longer route. That wasn't what I wanted, and we gave up trying to beat just staying on U.S. 64 to Morganton. I went to bed after again eating just about everything in sight. There was a great convenience store beside the motel and a McDonald's across the road. The forecast for Saturday included another chance of rain and snow, but I was used to both by now.

After another quiet night, I was excited to get the motel breakfast, which the owner had said would be ready by 5:30 a.m. I arrived at the front door and found it locked and the desk unattended. I tapped on the door, and the owner came running around the corner in the clothes he had worn to bed. His first words were an apology when I asked about the breakfast. He said he only needed 10 more minutes to finish it, so I went back to the room to finish packing. The breakfast was ready when I returned, as much as he had put out, but I never saw him again. It was time to head to Chimney Rock and Lake Lure!

With the snow gone and only a few clouds to dim the sunrise, the radio announcer reported snow to the north and the weather reporter at a local station warned listeners to watch out for flurries. The first three miles heading east were mostly on wide and nearly new sidewalks. Of course, that came to an end as I left Hendersonville behind and found the white line at the edge of the pavement again. Still, early Saturday morning traffic was not too bad, but I again spent plenty of time off the road.

I had heard that Hendersonville was apple country but didn't remember ever driving through it before. Edneyville must be the apple packing capital of North Carolina. Large packing buildings and orchards took up much of the road frontage. There was only one stoplight and it was close to a school, probably used more for student dropoff than anything else. The busiest business on that Saturday morning was a convenience store with a grill in it, which must have been the local meeting place. There was even outdoor seating for a warmer time. I used it while eating one of my egg and cheese biscuits. While there, I asked about some friends from the area who were my fellow students at Western Carolina. One guy, the leader of the group named Mike Dunlap, got a few nods but no one knew where he was now. They didn't know Steve Whitaker and David Parris. All of these guys played on our dorm's intramural football team, on which I served as quarterback. We played flag football, and if I was the quarterback, this surely meant that we didn't have much going for us. But if I could get the ball close to Parris, he would catch it and use his speed to outrun everybody else. We even won a few games with that connection.

The traffic got even lighter as I journeyed on. The upcoming section had me worried because the roads quickly become curvy and had no shoulders for miles. I had dreaded the route to Lake Lure since checking out the area by truck a few weeks ahead of the journey. My hope was that cold weather and the weekend might lessen the traffic from an average day.

The next settlement ahead was Bat Cave, and by the time I arrived, I was just walking along, dodging traffic and listening to music when I noticed a man standing beside the road up ahead who appeared to be waiting for me. He was looking straight at me like he had something on this mind. Marvin Fisher of Hendersonville wanted to know about my trip and how I came to be out here on the road that morning. His daughter owns the Esmerelda Lodge and Restaurant nearby, and Marvin does some work for her. While talking to him, I noticed a carload of folks who nodded and waved as they prepared to leave what looked like a woodworking shop. Those folks would become more significant shortly in a series of coincidences.

I waved good-bye to everyone and headed toward Chimney Rock. Along the way, I noticed the very impressive Esmerelda Lodge and realized that I should have asked Marvin for a good deal on a high-end room. "Our State" magazine had recently posted a big ad for the place. I did notice another small motel owner who came out and took his vacancy sign down and proceeded to lock the office. Not a car was in sight at his motel, meaning that I had missed out on that one. After all, March was still considered off-season.

# CHAPTER 4

*Chimney Rock and coming down*
*out of the mountains — Stopping by home*

. . . . . . . . . . . . . . . . . . . . . . . . . . . . . . . . . . . . . . . . . . .

One of my favorite locations previously visited in this area was Lake Lure. I had spent a few days there when my youngest daughter, Amber, got married the first time. I remembered from that trip how hard it was to run once you got away from the flat part of town. During that trip, I tried to run up the hill toward Chimney Rock and didn't enjoy it much. The good thing was that this time, I was fortunate enough to have a steady downhill grade into Chimney Rock and that would continue on into Lake Lure the next day.

As I entered Chimney Rock Village, I noticed that the town seemed jammed full of tourists and that almost every available parking place was full. My plan was to climb to the top of the actual Chimney Rock this time and see the view that I had never experienced. My goal was to make it to the top, come down and grab some food, find my planned motel and watch a basketball game. All of that seemed doable from my point of view.

I knew it would be a long climb to go up the Chimney Rock Road but I didn't realize just how long. Two signs caught my attention, one of them stating that no bikes or pedestrians were allowed. I saw two people walking way ahead of me so I kept on going. The other sign stated that tickets and information were available a mile ahead. I just kept on going.

Remember the folks who waved at me from the wood-working shop? As I climbed up the road, they were coming down and stopped to talk. They told me that the climb to the top was more like three miles, way past the ticket booth. The road was too steep to try to run, and I realized that a walk to the top would take an hour. It would take me another hour to get back down in addition to the viewing time at the top. My new friends told me that the elevator to the top wasn't working so that would be another climb and I couldn't take the stroller. That part didn't bother me much but time had become a concern. The basketball game was important because I have had season tickets to Davidson College's games for years. This year, the team was good but overachieving lately and had a shot to make the A-10 Tournament Finals. In order to do so, they had to win on this day.

I chose to save the view from the top of Chimney Rock State Park for another day. Back on U.S. 64, I headed east to find my room but almost immediately found my four new friends enjoying their rocking chairs. Rota and Rod Hessenius of Fletcher, N.C., and Judy and Clayton Henrichsen of Spencer, Iowa, introduced themselves, and we caught up on a few things. I didn't expect to see them again after this third meeting within just over an hour in a crowded tourist town.

My time was wasting away, and I wanted to find my room. The previous evening, I had called a few places and all of their prices were higher than I liked to pay. When I scoffed at $100 a night, one clerk suggested that I call the Riverside Lodge. I did call and managed to get a room for about half that price and hoped it would be OK. After leaving my friends, I asked Siri for directions to the Riverside Lodge, and as had become too common, her directions were wrong and would have had me going the other way back west. I knew I hadn't passed the lodge so I stopped at a very nice bakery and asked to make sure. They had baked goods galore, and I was starving. Both women working there took great pleasure in talking to me and giving directions, so I realized I had to buy some cookies. I went back in and purchased some of the best oatmeal raisin cookies — my favorite kind — that I've ever had. I only ate one right then, planning to enjoy the rest while watching the game.

With only about an hour before the game, I found the Riverside Lodge. It wasn't quite as nice as some of the other places but had a very pleasant staff, especially the clerk in the office, who was confined to a wheelchair. I asked him about WiFi, which I needed because I didn't have much of a phone signal and knew I would have to send my story later. The clerk said the WiFi was spotty at best but depending on the weather, he felt that one corner of a nearby room was near enough to the office to receive pretty good reception. In fact, once I had paid, he let me go see what kind of reception I got in two rooms. Neither of the rooms had a good signal on that afternoon, and I went back and told him so. Next, he suggested that I go across the back parking lot to the Tiki Lounge and see if it was better there. The signal still wasn't good enough to transmit a picture, and I went back to the office. One of the workers tried to help me and then another one joined in. Nothing worked, so knowing that my story submission deadline was coming up soon, I asked for my money back and called the higher priced place from last night's conversation. Yes, she agreed to still give me a big discount, but the cost would still be almost $100.

I headed back west to find my new lodging, but not without yet another encounter with the Hessenius and Henrichsen families as they were coming out of a gift shop. One of the guys said, "But what about your game?" I told them about my hunt for WiFi and said, "I still have a few minutes!" before hustling on up the road. That jovial group had to be tired of seeing me. As it turned out, the eastern end of the village was a dead zone for all my electronics but everything improved slightly as I moved toward the center of town.

The employees at the new place didn't have the same personalities as the staff at the Riverside Lodge, but the room was a little nicer and had a spectacular balcony overlooking the river. The WiFi worked great so I was in business as far as my newspaper reporting. I turned on the TV, couldn't find the game but was able to get it on my iPad. I settled in to do my story and listen to what would hopefully be a Wildcat victory. Things had finally settled down, and my oatmeal raisin cookies hit the spot. The bad thing was that I had not taken time to get more food, and my bags were nearly empty.

The Wildcats did win and were set to play for the conference championship on Sunday, a game that would also be televised. The story and great pictures from my day's journey transmitted well, and I enjoyed some time watching the cold river flow by just below my balcony. From start to finish, I had only covered 20 miles today and was OK with that. Tomorrow would be a bigger challenge. Another cold rain was in the forecast, and the Davidson win added an unusual challenge. I knew the next game would be held early Sunday afternoon and I had some tough climbing and sharp curves ahead of me as I rose out of the Lake Lure basin en route to Rutherfordton. I put off planning for Sunday until I found some more food.

When I went inside, Chimney Rock Village was booming with people, and there were vehicles everywhere. When I came back out at about 6 p.m., almost everyone was gone and most of the stores and shops were closed or closing soon. Because of that, I faced the challenge of finding some reasonably priced food. What I did find was one incredible story that still seems amazing as I write this book almost two months later.

I looked around for anything that was open where I could get some food. A couple of bar and grill establishments were still open, and one seemed to be doing a pretty good business, so I decided to go inside. I hadn't taken much care to clean up and didn't have any clothes that were completely clean anyway. Even though I probably looked like a vagrant when I stepped inside, one of the young waitresses was all smiles and asked me if I was alone. I told her I was and just wanted to get a take-out order. She gave me a menu and asked several friendly questions, so I ended up telling her about my walk/run across the state. She said, "Can I go? I would love to do something like that." Having seen quite a bit on the road by now, I was surprised to hear this very attractive woman in her mid-20s make such a request. I was also surprised to find a veggie burger on the menu and ordered it while our conversation continued. I think her name was Julie, but I can't be sure. She obviously was not really busy and began to tell me about spending her teen years in California. Living with an aunt, Julie had been so unhappy she decided to either take her life or leave the house and start hitchhiking.

She chose to begin a life of hitchhiking and living out of dumpsters. "No one ever bothered me," she said, "and

I actually gained weight. You wouldn't believe what stores throw out and how much there is. The place I have seen that throws out the most food is Trader Joe's. They throw out tons of stuff." I was mesmerized by her story and enjoyed listening to her. Julie wanted to know more about me and started asking questions about my life. She seemed to enjoy the stories of my bike trips and said she still wanted to see the rest of the world. I asked about her job and whether she liked it and planned to stay. Julie said, "Yes, I like it, and it is still cold so I will stay for at least a while. Plus, I met a guy a few weeks ago who I sort of like, but I don't know if he would like to travel with me."

With that, my order arrived and we continued to talk a little more. We hugged and wished each other "safe travels," and then we both said "Goodbye!" The next time I drive through Chimney Rock Village, I will stop in and see if she's still there. I'm betting that she won't be.

Back at the room, I came up with a plan for Sunday, my eighth day on the road and possibly the most challenging yet. I was sticking to U.S. 64, which made the route easy, but I wanted to make it to Rutherfordton and get a motel before the Davidson game came on TV. Significant rain and a good chance of some snow mixed in were in the forecast, predicted to likely begin overnight. I went to bed, full of food and thinking of both Julie's story and the day ahead that would begin very soon. I planned to leave quite early and travel for several hours in the dark.

Up at 4:45 a.m. and excited about the day ahead, I looked out to see a dry road. Rain was still in the forecast but had not yet started. My feet hit the pavement at 5:30, the first day of daylight saving time so the cloudy morning would likely have three more hours of darkness before dawn. If it started to rain, the darkness could be worse, but I hoped for the best.

Heading east toward Lake Lure was mostly downhill, and I had the road to myself as you might expect. My red flashing light was only turned on when a car was approaching, helping to save the hard-to-change batteries. I passed the part of Lake Lure that borders on U.S. 64 and saw again that the water level was still way down for lake and property repairs. At least once as I climbed back uphill after leaving Lake Lure, I had to use my cell phone to light up a sign confirming that U.S. 64 was turning. Still, my trek in the dark was going well, and rain still hadn't started. The eastern sky began to brighten and a little more traffic joined me but not enough to cause any concern.

Daylight finally arrived and about halfway to Rutherfordton, light rain began falling. I passed a small motel midway between Lake Lure and Rutherfordton, one which I had seen on my drive to check out the route. Though it was far from any store, it looked quite inviting but I decided to keep going as the rain began to intensify. I was determined to push hard through the rain and make it to Rutherfordton's only motel, at least the only one I could find on my map.

I was a little concerned because I had called the Dog-wood Motel probably more than five times the previous night with no answer. Still, I felt mildly confident that I would find it open because it had plenty of cars on my fact-finding trip and lots of so/so reviews. The others in the area were at least four to six miles away, and I was already cold and wet after 23 miles through the long morning.

About this time, just as the heavy rain started, a big guy in an even bigger pickup truck stopped to see if I wanted a ride. He had turned around and came back to block traffic while he asked. His offer was tempting but as always, I had to turn it down, although the ride would have taken me most of the way to the motel. Later, I saw him pass by again going in the opposite direction.

I arrived at the Dogwood Motel in Rutherfordton at 12:30 p.m., with 30 minutes to spare before the game. The owner told me the motel had been full until just an hour before and said a room would be available as soon as the staff finished cleaning it. She suggested that I just sit and wait, but sitting doesn't come easy to me until I can become comfortable. The rain had found ways to soak into my clothes and I needed to get warm, so I just stood and waited.

The room was prepared within about 15 minutes, and I had already discovered that the WiFi worked well. My only concerns now were that the room was suitable and that the TV worked. Surely it would have CBS, the channel on which the game was scheduled to be televised. With 10 minutes to spare, I was in a heated room and ready to settle down. A convenience store was just 500 feet away, but there would be time to visit it later.

Davidson won again and all went well for a restful afternoon. As my wet clothes dried on the heater, I warmed up quickly, too. I began to plan for my trip to Morganton on Monday, another day likely to start out with rain and a chance of snow. Caught up and quite cozy, I went to bed early.

This time, the predicted rain did happen and by 4:30 a.m., I could hear it from my room. I looked out and saw the rain pouring. This was a cold rain, but I closed the door and got dressed to go. I already knew that the road didn't have a shoulder as far as the convenience store and I could see that traffic was heavy already. The fleeting thought of spending another night passed very quickly as it was not a habit that I wanted to start. About 7:40, I hit the road in what was probably the heaviest rain and worst traffic. My rain gear had been doing well, but it would be tested yet again. Some available daylight made me feel safer than I probably was.

The first mile was the worst single part of my journey because I was all the way off the road and getting rained on and splashed regularly by a solid line of oncoming traffic. As usual when in the toughest of situations, I took time for a brief prayer. Plugging on, I found that the next mile was at least as bad before two miraculous things happened. I passed by an elementary school where parents were dropping off their kids and heading back toward me. But once past the school, the traffic was at least cut by half and then half again by both U.S. 74A and 221 turning and exiting off of U.S. 64.

Suddenly I was facing minimal traffic and a little more daylight followed by a slightly wider shoulder. My prayer was answered yet again. The rain didn't let up but I counted that as the least of my worries. Soon, the rain turned into a cold and wind-driven snow. For the first time on the journey, the wind was blowing in my face, making my hands even colder. Even though I was wearing mittens wrapped in plastic bags, I couldn't keep my hands warm.

My hands were so cold that I had inserted the Hot Hands warming packets that I purchased at the Horseshoe hardware store. They were not the same as the ones I usually bought, and although larger, were not effective. I began to pray again for a solution and just a few minutes later, the only convenience store I had seen all morning came into view. Once I saw that store, I began praying that it would carry the good quality Hot Hands.

Drawing stares from the four customers in the store, I walked in and saw the clerk making a pizza. Without asking, I looked around, noticing that the store had a couple shelves of hardware-type products, but most of the spaces were either empty or close to it. On the last shelf, I spotted a full box of Hot Hands and thanked God for answering yet another of my prayers. The pizza-making clerk took my money and said, "I didn't even know we had those." It is so cool the way that God looks after me on these trips!

My hands were warm for the rest of the day, reminding me of the fork and spoon incident on the Washington state to Wisconsin bike ride. After breaking one of the plastic tire tools used to separate the bike rim from the tire, I was several days away from a bike shop. I saw a metal fork beside the road and passed it by before realizing that the top of the handle would work well as a replacement. I thought, "If God put that there for me, then He will do it again." And right away, I found a metal spoon, once again perfect for the job.

I pushed the jogger on east through some more snow later in the morning and then partly cloudy skies in the afternoon. The road shoulder was better, too, on a freshly paved road that had packed gravel neatly formed to the side of the asphalt. It was good for running a wheel or two off the pavement when needed.

Some of the most spectacular scenery of the journey was on this rolling section of the road. I saw restored old farm houses scattered along the beautiful mountains, some of them shining white with snow. I stopped to see some interesting animals during the day, including a couple of miniature horses and a burro that all came over to me, wanting attention. Maybe they just wanted to be fed, but either way,

I hadn't talked to a person since the clerk at the store where I bought the Hot Hands. A herd of longhorn cattle didn't seem to care for me and hardly looked up.

A human and some humor caught up to me just a few minutes later. I needed to take a bathroom break really bad when I spotted one of those little telephone buildings. I pushed the jogger up to the front of it and walked behind the building to ease off the pressure. Just as I had zipped up my pants and walked around to the front, a telephone truck backed up to the jogger. While I acted as if I hadn't been caught, Jonathan Duncan of Morganton didn't say a word and went about unloading something from his truck. I broke the ice and told him about my adventure, and his first response was "Why?" My answer took a good bit longer to explain. We shared a few laughs, and I headed on toward Morganton.

Along the way, I found plenty of history. The famous Revolutionary War Battle of Kings Mountain was preceded by a skirmish at Canes Creek between Loyalists and the "Overmountain Men." The creek had been walled up by stones at some time over the years and was quite beautiful. The skirmish happened in 1780, and Fort McGaughey was constructed nearby. All of this was listed on several historical markers.

My goal for the day was to make it to the Interstate 40 side of Morganton and meet Amber. I was able to find her after 30 miles, load up the baby jogger, and head for home to meet several community commitments. By moving my "cross the state" adventure until early in March, I had to make two of these trips back home for different events in China Grove and Salisbury. When I sat down in her car, I knew that my legs were still sore and that I had been pushing the pace not only for that day but for the whole trip. Two days of healing and rest would be a good thing.

Once home, I met those commitments and took time to repack my gear. Originally, I had planned to leave behind some of my cold weather clothing. However, based on the lingering cold and upcoming forecast, I decided not to leave anything behind. All of the clothing got washed and reloaded, along with plenty of Hot Hands packets. Snow was in the long-range forecast again.

My good friend and fellow runner, Wayne Crowder, had offered to take me back to the same spot in Morganton on Thursday morning. He picked me up very early so that I could start running in Morganton by daylight. Two highlights of my time at home had been the start of my beginning runners class at Novant Health Rowan Medical Center, our local hospital, and making a presentation to the Salisbury Lions Club. Both had gone extremely well. I was super excited to get on the road again. This portion of the journey would include following U.S. 70 to Statesville and then to home, where I would again take time out to fulfill commitments. This would be a three-day push on slightly more familiar roads and would include the towns of Drexel,

Valdese, Rutherford College, Connelly Springs, Icard and Long View.

As I pushed through Morganton, the sidewalks and some shoulders made the road very passable. I stopped to load my bags with some snacks and found the cold morning turning into a perfect mid-morning, with plenty of sun and a gentle tailwind. It was great to be pushing the baby jogger down the road again. Plenty of drivers made sure they gave me enough room and many waved, both acts of kindness helping to make for a fun morning.

The first real town I came to was Valdese, another place that meant a lot to me. Another of my college roommates was from Valdese, and I realized that I was remembering these guys a long time past when I should have. Ronnie Annas was a great guy who helped me get through that first year at Western Carolina. Valdese is a very cool and well-kept town that has a great looking dairy bar that would have been much more tempting on a slightly warmer day.

Two unusual things happened that morning that caught my attention. One lady who was driving toward me slowly with no other traffic close by kept motioning toward me and the side of the road. She seemed older and nicely dressed but it appeared that she didn't want me using her road. The next thing was a car with two women in it who seemed to be filming me on a large video camera as they drove closer. I think I saw the same car a few minutes later parked across the road along the edge of a parking lot. After that, I never saw them again. It is fun to look into the cars at the drivers and passengers when I am not particularly worried about the traffic.

I did meet two fine people that morning along the road. One was Jeff Johnson, a phone lineman who was working beside U.S. 70. Jeff was a native of Avery County and said he had enjoyed the milder winters at his new home in Hickory. He also gave me some pointers on where I could stay that night and had good reasons why. Our nice conversation ended just as I noticed that the temperature was starting to warm and I thought about taking off my long pants soon, a pleasant thought.

Just a little way on down the road near Connelly Springs, I noticed that a car had turned around and appeared to be waiting for me in a parking lot. As it turned out, Wayne Collins lived nearby and was interested in my jogging stroller and wanted to know if I could put pedals on it. Recumbent bikes (on which the rider sits down and leans backward) do look much like the pro-style Baby Jogger brand. Oftentimes on this trip, I had thought about how much easier riding and pedaling would be. Mr. Collins also talked about his current project, making a pull-behind trailer out of a 55-gallon barrel that could haul kids. I told him that he should go visit Michelle at Patterson Farms near my home and that she could show him a whole trailer of them that are painted to resemble Holstein cows. Mr. Collins had said he didn't want to hold me up, but we both took turns restarting the conversation.

After quite a bit of uncertainty, I ended up spending the night at the Budget Inn in Hickory. I had heard from Jeff Johnson that the place was OK, but asked again at the nearby Dollar General. Both store workers told me to stay away, and one of them shared a bad experience she had there. I listened and they called a couple of other places, one that was off route and another that was quite a bit higher. I chose to take a chance and stay at the Budget Inn. It didn't start off well.

The Davidson Wildcats were playing again on TV that night, and I wanted to make sure that I would be able to watch the NCAA tournament. After reading several bad reviews, I asked one of the owners to see the room before I paid. The outside of the motel looked fine, but the room they showed me was just adequate and had an entrance door that didn't close tightly. However, the price was right. I went back and paid for the room, even though the owner's daughter wanted me to pay in cash to get the quoted price. I hadn't heard that before and told her I wouldn't do cash, and she agreed to put it on my card. I went back to my room with food and settled in to watch the game.

Just after the game started, the power went off in my room. I ran back to the office, and the owner was back at the desk. I told him what had happened, and he tossed me a key to another room, hollering, "You should have told me that you don't smoke. This is a non-smoking room!" I ran back to my first room, grabbed everything and went to the new room and thought I had moved to the Marriott. The two rooms were as different as night and day. Everything in it was first class, and the TV was much better. I counted all of this as a stroke of luck at the end of a fairly easy 24-mile day, highlighted by an afternoon tailwind.

The hills had lessened and should continue to do so. I felt good at the end of the day, except for the fact that Davidson lost to Kentucky in a close game and ended its season. My day ended with a hot shower, after which I went to bed early in the nice room. I still couldn't believe my luck on the power going out.

With the days slowly starting to lengthen, I was back on the road by 7:30 and facing moderate traffic. I stopped at McDonald's early and grabbed some cookies and two egg and cheese McMuffins — "hold the sausage, please" — to power my morning. Early on, I encountered mostly good shoulders and lighter traffic, but the traffic continued to get heavier as more folks rolled into Hickory. The first point of history was the Hickory Motor Speedway, home of NASCAR racing legends Ned and Dale Jarrett. I crossed the road and walked over for a closer look. The very busy schedule for 2018 was posted on the wall of the historic race track.

Another sunny and moderate day had become quite comfortable by mid-morning as I tried to figure out how to navigate through Newton-Conover. The best thing was that the 321 Highway turned away from U.S. 70. Afterwards, I had the corner of the road mostly to myself as traffic was very light. I passed through Claremont and headed toward some beautiful countryside.

The absolute best experience of the trip so far occurred next as I found the Bunker Hill Covered Bridge, one of the last two such bridges in North Carolina. It was located just a short 500 yards off U.S. 70, and I took time to go see it. The bridge was built in an old-fashioned barn raising by local farmers in 1894. Still very solid all these years later, the bridge was blocked off to cars but has a nice park around it.

I walked on a gravel sidewalk to get to the bridge. A woman and a small boy were the only ones on the bridge when I got there. I noticed that the bridge was solid and looked like it could easily still support a car. I made some photos and got ready to go. Just about that time, I noticed a happy looking couple walking onto the bridge. David Frazier and his soon-to-be wife, Amy, were stopping by the bridge at the last minute while on their way to their wedding. David had proposed there on a snowy December afternoon, and they said it felt only right to make one last visit before they got married. We talked for a while, and I found out that they are both runners, too, and they wanted to know all about my journey. When they said they needed to go, I wished them a wonderful wedding and a happy life together.

On toward Statesville, I noticed Randy Stewart working

on his racing go kart. Randy was immediately friendly and told me not to worry about his dogs. Though loud, he said they were not dangerous. Randy told me about the kart and asked about my journey. He offered to let me sit in the kart, and I, of course, accepted. I had no idea how hard it would be to get in the small cockpit, especially since Randy was bigger than me. My legs and tired body weren't the most pliable at that time, but Randy helped me. Finally, I got in and Randy made some photos while telling me that it was best for the kart to fit tight, especially since they can go over 100 mph on the right tracks. Randy said getting in the kart takes the right technique and that he was hesitant to buy it without trying to get in first.

More North Carolina counties of Macon, Jackson, Transylvania, Henderson, Rutherford, Burke, Catawba and soon-to-be Iredell would have been in my rear-view mirror if I had one.

While I pushed the jogger quite late into the day, I arrived at the Motel 7 in Statesville with a total of 33 miles, $0.20 found on the road and very large amount of screws and nails pitched off the pavement. I had enjoyed the people and nice weather and was just a day's run/walk from home. I was sore, suffering from nagging tenderness and had an uncertain motel ahead. Still, it had been another great day on the road!

# CHAPTER 5

*Nearing halfway and still more snow —*
*Plenty of friends on the road, some old and some new*

. . . . . . . . . . . . . . . . . . . . . . . . . . . . . . . . . . . . . . . . . . . . . . . . . . .

T he first thing I did when I checked in at the Motel 7 was to take a good look at my surroundings. The desk clerk was working his first day. The female manager seemed to know everything about the motel, including how to make an excuse or two. I had stopped at another motel at the U.S. 70 and Interstate 77 exit and found the price quite high. The only one that wasn't a major chain, at least I didn't think it was, happened to be the Motel 7.

I asked to see the room first and told the housekeeper who took me to see it that I just wanted a quiet room and a good TV to watch basketball that night. She said she understood and showed me what she called one of the best rooms still available. While the building looked modern and was multi-story, the rooms looked quite worn, and none of the TVs were flat screens. I already had been given a good price but thought of leaving and checking out the Motel 6 which was close by. The housekeeper told me that she used to live and work there but left because transients and shady types frequented the place. Then she said, "I tell you what, I have a 55-inch flat screen TV in my room and will let you have it for tonight if you decide to stay with us. We have had lots of flat screen TVs stolen over the last few weeks, but you are welcome to use mine tonight if you want. My boyfriend will even hook it up for you."

She went down with me to the front desk and confirmed the deal. The manager said it was OK, and the housekeeper left to get the TV set up. To give them time to do it, I went to the nearby Waffle House and got an omelet, a waffle and some hash browns. I wasn't worried too much about the motel and knew that I could get through a night just about anywhere, especially since the next night would be spent in my own bed if all went well.

With darkness coming soon, I climbed the stairs on the outside to get to my room and found the housekeeper and her boyfriend finishing up on installing the TV. It was huge and worked great! Just as I had most nights, I submitted my story, caught up on messages, ate a ton and took a hot shower. I slept great and hardly heard a sound in the motel. I didn't have to worry about anybody bothering me the whole night. Still sore in my left shin area, I could not run far and expected to be walking most of the next day toward home.

Up again with first light, I headed onto U.S. 70 and moved into the left lane with no shoulder. With little traffic, I was fine but the vehicles seemed to have a hard time seeing me. Twice, I jumped the curb to avoid a vehicle passing too closely, Having had only a light pastry for breakfast, I looked forward to getting back to my farm and settled into an easy pace that wouldn't bother my shin.

Not ten minutes into the day's journey, I was surprised to see Kenneth Todd hop out of a truck and run over to join me. Kenneth lives in a housing development across the woods from my farm, and we often see each other on early morning runs. He works for Del Monte and is an ultramarathoner, meaning that he loves the really long distances. Kenneth had read that I would be following U.S. 70 back toward home and decided to spend the morning running with me. Since I couldn't run that day, he was gracious enough to walk with me for almost 10 miles. Kenneth had told me that he plans to do a similar route across the state in the next year. His will be different from mine in that his trek will be for total time while pushing to beat the fastest known journey across the state. Kenneth told me he hopes to average about 45 miles a day. He plans to use Jay, another neighbor, to support him in the effort by traveling ahead and arranging for lodging, food and any other needs. "And I won't be stopping to talk to the people along the way like you do!" Kenneth said. So our journeys were going to be similar in some ways but very different in others.

Most of the time between Statesville and Cleveland, we talked about the things and people that I had seen and met, including various road conditions that were especially challenging. Kenneth wouldn't be pushing a baby jogger either nor could I imagine covering that many miles a day. For whatever help it will provide, Kenneth will get one of my first books once it is published. I wish him the best and hope he breaks the record.

Kenneth caught a ride home with Jay and headed to a church breakfast fundraiser near there while I stopped by the H&B Market in Cleveland to use the bathroom and grab some snacks. BeBe, the owner, was excited to hear about my trip and gathered her family and staff around for a group photo. It was fun to meet them and share about the long journey.

I was back in Salisbury Post country and Rowan County, and I had thought there might be a few people stopping by on the roads toward home. My old friends, Dan and Sandy Pflughaupt, found me just as soon as I left the market. They brought Reese's Cups and a couple pairs of gloves for the cold mornings still to come. Sandy used to work with me at a distribution center, and Dan serviced material handling equipment at another plant. They had also purchased hay from my farm over the years. Sandy even kept a traveling pet zoo for a while and always enjoys her animals. Dan has been with Aldi for a while now and seems quite happy there. We made plans to meet for breakfast after all this was done and I had a chance to catch up at home.

A steady stream of friends began to stop by, all familiar with where I would be today from my articles in the

Salisbury Post. Mike and Debbie Long stopped by on their way to a day trip in the mountains, and I told them to visit Valdese if they hadn't already. Mike was previously the long-time youth minister and Debbie sang in the choir at my church in China Grove. She also worked for years with the N.C. Department of Corrections. They eventually continued on, and so did I. I got off U.S. 70 onto N.C. 801 and passed West Rowan High School after which Buddy Hoffner pulled over. Buddy owns Hoffner Organic Dairy Farm just about three miles from my farm. Just minutes later, Emory and Susan Graham also stopped. All three have been nearly lifelong friends, and I count them as the type of easy and comfortable neighbors who I can miss seeing for months and still ease back into great conversation. Buddy, Emory and I played on the same softball team for many years, and our friendships deepened during that time. All three remain very active, with Susan and Emory enjoying bike rides together and a new juice diet.

Just a quarter mile later, David Ketner — who some consider the world's greatest Red Sox fan — was the next to stop. Being a diehard Yankees fan, I consider being a long-time Red Sox fan something closer to a wasted life, but David always wants to get me a shirt. He is still laughing about the time another friend got me an authentic Red Sox cap, one of the really good ones if there is such a thing. It was all done as a joke, and I am not ashamed to say that it took me weeks to give it away. No real American North Carolinian would want such a thing! David was another member of the same softball team and is the public works manager for the Town of China Grove. With David blocking one side of the road with his motorcycle, another neighbor, Phil Dwiggins, stopped by in the Locke Fire Department tanker truck. He blocked the other side of the rural road, which didn't have much demand anyway. Phil works for the state road maintenance department.

I began to think that I wouldn't get home until I could hide in the dark but genuinely enjoyed seeing all these great folks. All these relationships matter more to me than any material things. Almost home, I ran up Weaver Road and surprised my across-the-road neighbor, Ollie McKnight. "You came all the way from Statesville already?" she asked. While it wasn't particularly fast, I wouldn't have changed a thing about all the morning's interactions. What had been a very cool day ended with what turned out to be the most fun 21 miles of the trip.

Over the next two days, I would try to heal the shin splint with some ice and rest and work on a blister, the first of my trip. I was scheduled to work at church on Sunday, and the final visit for a study at the Appalachian State University Performance Lab was set for very early Tuesday. I would be back on the road shortly afterwards. I counted this day as about halfway for the journey although the actual halfway point would not happen until I was close to Lexington on Tuesday.

I was itching to get going again and finished my final testing at the performance lab by 7:50 a.m. on Tuesday. In a moderate hurry, I got home just in time to load my stroller and pre-packed bags in the back of Ollie McKnight's truck. She had agreed to take me to where I turned off U.S. 70 onto 801. After giving her a quick goodbye hug, I headed east on 70 and a late morning return to U.S. 64. Willie Nelson's tune "On the Road Again!" never sounded so good. The blister was a lot better, but the shin only moderately so.

My only stop during the morning happened just after I had passed through Woodleaf and then Cooleemee, two very small towns that I see quite often. One of my favorite convenience stores in the area is at what used to be called "Greasy Corners," which is located at the intersection of 801 and 601. I once heard the name came from the fact that several barbecue joints and gas stations were located at the intersection. The convenience store is by far the best thing happening there these days.

When I did finally reach the intersection of U.S. 64 and N.C. 801, I truly felt that the journey had resumed. Though traffic had been very light on the 801 portion of the morning, I didn't expect the same on 64, and it wasn't. Somehow "dreaded" makes a perfect fit when used in conjunction with rumble strips, those deep carved asphalt enemies of cyclists and now baby joggers. I picked up dreaded rumble strips as soon as I turned toward Lexington and rejoined U.S. 64.

Traffic was heavy, with lots of trucks, and the rumble

DAVID FREEZE

strips forced me onto the wet and lumpy grass for most of the next 10 miles. It was cold, too, and a couple of friends later told me that they had seen me on the road that day. I was bundled up and looked larger than I am.

Not much happened during that portion of the day except for my ongoing frustration with being forced off the road. There was no running again. I did see a very interesting pulpwood operation with some nice equipment near where the Daniel Boone Canoe Trail crossed underneath U.S. 64 on the Yadkin River. Daniel Boone had spent a large portion of his life in our area before heading off to fame in Kentucky.

Thinking back on how I chose to use N.C. 801 as the connector to rejoin U.S. 64, the decision hadn't come easily. It seemed that everyone I asked about it had a different opinion. Kenneth Todd and Buddy Hoffner weighed in and seemed to make the most sense on the subject because the ease of traffic and lack of complications offered a match with one of the shortest routes. I believe they were right, and since they agreed with me, that was good enough.

Once I reached Lexington, there were just two goals on my mind. The first, of course, was to find some food. I bypassed a grocery store to stop at a Subway, for which a new gift card was burning a hole in my pocket and needed to be used. I ordered a large sandwich, some cookies and a bag of chips, confident that these calories would be enough because there were still some food items in my bag. After ordering about $10 worth of food, I asked for a large cup of water. The clerk told me that the cup would cost $2.50, no matter what I put in it. She went on to explain that this was the owner's rule. As a frequent traveler and Subway fan, I had never heard of this and told her so. In fact, my comment was something like, "Did that cup actually cost you 3 cents?" She softened up and said, "Probably not even that." That swung the argument and I got the cup, just as I should have. This was by far my longest conversation of the day and not worth a picture.

Next up was getting to a motel. The forecast had deteriorated throughout the day, and the area was under a snow watch overnight and throughout the next morning. Plus, it was continuing to get colder. I called one motel a couple of times and only got a message. The other place I was considering had some less-than-nice reviews but the price was wonderful. My motto is "I can make it through one night anywhere!" as I have proven before many times. I headed to the Budget Inn.

The motel looked fine from outside, and I saw the clerk filling a bucket from the ice machine. She gave me the good price that I had expected, and I paid for the room. Once inside, I found a room that was not the cleanest I had seen. However, I became even more concerned when I turned on the heater and nothing seemed to happen. It was an old electric baseboard heater and had been left unplugged. The room wasn't much warmer than it was outside, and I was ready for some heat. After five minutes, I still couldn't feel any heat and called the office, after which someone was dispatched to look at it. That person, a resident of one of the other rooms, told me that his was the same kind and worked fine after a while, but he said, "Don't open the door!" I waited and it did finally begin to work but I was so cold that I never took a shower. On the flip side, the TV channel selection was spectacular!

My thoughts turned to the next day and how to use Business Interstate 85 to access U.S. 64 as I headed southwest toward Asheboro. I doubted that a man and a stroller were supposed to use the interstate, especially if it was snowing. Finally, I called it a day after 30 miles in a slightly warmer room than it had been outside late that afternoon. I had not opened the door.

I did open the door the next morning to check the actual weather conditions. Snow was falling and the temperature actually seemed a little warmer, maybe because of less wind. Snow was accumulating on the cars and a little on the grass, but nothing on the roads.

Dressing quickly and feeling fine as I got ready to leave the room, I headed out the door. I could see the interstate from the door and the traffic rushing by. There seemed to be no choice but to use the busy road. I had no trouble giving it a try but fully expected to see flashing blue lights directed at me. Instead of entering against traffic because of the fenced-off median, I chose to take the opposite side and run with traffic. And run I did, at the fastest rate of the journey so far. There was no real shoulder because of construction and at one time, I was actually in the lane with traffic and low visibility because of snow and early light. Once again, after a few prayers on the run, God took care of me and I later exited off on U.S. 64 headed toward Asheboro.

The snow was heavy, and I listened to weather forecasts of continuous snow that morning and lessening amounts during the early afternoon. The shoulder at this point was very wide, and no cars or trucks got near me. The road was wet, but not slippery. All was going as well as could be expected on this unusual day.

The first motorist who stopped on the road jumped out to ask if I needed a ride. Glad that he was concerned, I hollered back that I was fine and wanted to do this on my own! I asked for a picture, and he immediately turned back to his vehicle, saying "No pictures!"

The second one turned around in the road in her very large, nice black pickup and also offered me a ride. When she heard that I was good and determined to stay after it, she seemed genuinely disappointed. "Good luck!" she said with a smile and a wave as she drove away.

About 10 miles out of Lexington, the road narrowed and the rumble strips were back. I had to again spend lots of time in the grass but the volume of traffic had lessened so that I could grab long segments of time in the traffic lane waiting for the next oncoming truck or car. I experienced pure joy when I would see a long line of traffic moving over as it came toward me, meaning that I could stay in the road.

Once I entered Randolph County, I got some more space. Knowing that I would be in Randolph all the way to Asheboro, I had hoped that the wider shoulders would continue. Most of the time, I could get the three wheels of the baby jogger on the pavement. The snow stopped and then changed to a light rain. Occasional wisps of blue sky peeked out and then covered over. For an hour or two, the air seemed to warm a little.

On my way into town, much of the last six miles seemed to be very hilly. This portion of Randolph County is part of the Uwharrie Mountains and includes the Uwharrie River. On a cold and cloudy day, the scenery reminded me of the Franklin and Brevard areas.

About 3 p.m., a sudden wind shift began to push from behind me, and sleet started to fall. Having already put away my heavy mittens, I got them and my still warm Hot Hands back out. They felt good as the temperature cooled rapidly. With the cold wind came a visit from a female deputy sheriff who stopped in the road to make sure I was OK. While other traffic stopped, I told her what I was doing and that I was enjoying the day. Way more attractive than the other law enforcement folks I had encountered so far, she laughed and shook her head, then drove away with a smile.

Almost immediately, I noticed that U.S. 64 was being widened and possibly rerouted. No vehicles could use the still under construction new road yet, but I did and it felt like a short break. Upon entering Asheboro, I stopped at an Exxon convenience store that was absolutely booming. One of the motorists at the pump was watching me so I stopped to talk. His name was David, too, and I asked about reasonable motels nearby. He suggested two that were coming up but leaned toward the new Motel 6. David also asked, "Where does the courage come from to do what you are doing? I have always wanted to do something like this but I am afraid of what might happen." I told him that I never worried, especially after praying over any tense situations and that I had grown to love these lasting adventures. I made his picture and headed toward the Motel 6, a chain with mostly good and a few lesser memories over the years.

After 30 miles tallied for the day, I stopped at the Glaze King Donuts store on the way to the motel. There, I met Sopha San, the owner, and picked out a few donuts. Usually, I am not a donut eater, but on these trips, all bets are off. Sopha's donuts looked great, except that the selection was very low at the end of the day. Starving, I picked out about five and packed them into my bags and told Sopha that I would mention her in my Salisbury Post article for the day.

The Motel 6 was just a block away. I stopped at the office and got a room, noticing that everything looked brand new. The office and my room were especially nice. Then I noticed the stairway and realized that it wasn't new. That is when I discovered a major renovation of an existing hotel underway that was in fact continuing next door. I loved the room and especially the heater that worked amazingly well. The motel was quiet with not too many patrons out and about.

Needing some more food after obliterating the donuts, I had seen from the hillside above the motel that some fast food places were just a road away. I couldn't figure how to get there until I walked through a construction area and came out on a road junction with plenty of food options available. A breakfast from McDonald's worked just fine.

The cold wasn't expected to break anytime soon, but I was still excited about seeing new cities and towns as I pushed toward the Outer Banks. Past Raleigh, I would be in a less frequented area, and of course, I had never seen any of it on foot. I asked my friend from home, Lt. Patrick Smith of the Salisbury Police Department, if he could contact someone from Cary and find out what to expect on road conditions once I got there. Cary and Raleigh would be the last biggest cities on the journey and both had interstates partnering with U.S. 64 through town in the direction that I would need to go. Rocky Mount might be an issue, too, but it was still up in the air.

I was tired, especially my legs, and of course, hungry all the time. The shin issue had improved some and nothing else really hurt. Early on Thursday morning, I just had to stop back by the Glaze King Donut shop and reload again. Every bit of the display space was crammed full of donuts and pastries, but I still took most of the same things that were so good the previous night. Sopha gave me a box to hold four items, and it was too big for my bag. I crunched the box up a little and was able to push it inside. I told Sopha that her picture was at the top of the online story in the Post but she hadn't seen it yet. I offered to show her but she said her kids would know how to access it. That suited me. I was ready to get back on the road.

It took four sometimes exasperating miles to get out of Asheboro. Traffic was inbound as I faced it and the times that I was against a curb with no shoulder didn't leave much room. Sometimes the back tire of the stroller actually rubbed against that curb. There were dozens of stoplights, too, often very long ones. I spent a lot of time standing and waiting, which was as hard to do as it is on a bicycle when passing through a long series of intersections. The considerate drivers and a few sidewalks helped.

Once I cleared the city limits, the wide shoulders returned. The fact that there were no rumble strips and gradually thinning traffic helped, too. Wide shoulders take the intensity out of traveling on foot or bike, and I sure experienced a less mentally challenging morning.

Another thing I liked about Randolph County was the fact that little trash was on or next to the roads. Some of the paving needed attention but it probably wasn't as rough when in a car. My time in Randolph had been mostly good, especially as I passed through Ramseur on sidewalks. I don't like sidewalks on a bike but love them on foot.

Wayne Crowder, my ride back to Morganton, had tipped me off to watch for Francis Bavier's grave as I entered Siler City. Bavier played Aunt Bee on the Andy Griffith show and helped provide plenty of memorable exchanges with Andy and Barney that are now cult classics. One of those shows was about the local pickle contest and how Aunt Bee tested her awful pickles on Andy, Opie and Barney. They kept on eating them because they hated to tell her how bad they were and that Clara's were much better. Fans of Aunt Bee had left jars of pickles on the very large headstone. Siler City was Bavier's chosen home, and she had remained there until her death in 1989. Siler City was only mentioned in one episode on the show, when Andy and Helen were caught for fishing without a license and had to go to court there. The cemetery is just a mile or so east of the start of the real town.

While nearing Siler City, I knew that my goal was to spend the night there, and I saw a good price online for the Days Inn. It was across town, which would add a couple miles in the right direction on a day that I felt really good. Both Siri and Google Assistant mentioned several motels, but they didn't mention the Siler City Motor Lodge, one of those Route 66-looking places that I like so much and was on the route. A man answered the phone right away when I called, and the price he quoted was excellent. When I called the Day's Inn, I was quoted a much higher price than the online one, and the woman at the front desk said she couldn't match it. I looked up the Siler City Motor Lodge, found nothing, but still had the confidence to give it a shot.

Ready to grab some food first, I stopped at the Best Food Cafeteria and Haley Bales Steakhouse. I didn't expect much because I am not a steakhouse person but I do know that the salads are often very good. The cafeteria had just opened when I went inside to meet Micah Boyd, who was running the register in a gift shop out front. She took me to the cafeteria and told me that the girls there would take care of me. I got a salad to go, based on how much I could get in a large take-out container. It's a good thing they didn't weigh it per pound like some places do now.

Somehow, I got the salad to sit almost level at the top of one of my bags and stopped at a convenience store for a good deal on large waters. I headed to the motor lodge and hoped things would continue to go well. My hot streak continued as I met the owner, who gave me my choice of two rooms to get the best WiFi. The rooms were old but very clean and just as I expected, the TV worked great and basketball was on that night. I had made just 24 miles for the day, but I knew that longer days were coming. Once in the room and attacking the huge salad, I thought back on some of my roadside finds of the day. It was a huge day coinwise, with three quarters and a nickel — $0.80 collected in all. I also found a size 13 very nice slip-on shoe and thought little of it until I found the perfect match about a mile farther down the road. I bet there was a story to tell about them as they looked brand new. Last but not least, I spotted a life-size Tweety Bird standing in the door of a home beside the road. I had to cross a four-lane road to get that picture.

Another cold night was forecast and a day with high temperatures in the 50s with little wind was on tap for Friday. It didn't sound super great, but it was the best forecast that I had heard in quite a while.

The miles were clicking by, and the baby jogger and I were about to hit the last third of the adventure. Hills were leveling out, and the ocean was getting closer. My body felt pretty good, my stomach was reasonably full, the shower was hot and the bed was firm. Daylight was starting to come earlier, a few clear days were in the forecast, and I was in my element. I couldn't be happier!

# CHAPTER 6

*Beginning the quest for the coast —*
*Fewer hills help with longer daily mileage*

. . . . . . . . . . . . . . . . . . . . . . . . . . . . . . . . . . . . . . . . . . . . . . .

The night in Siler City had been just what I needed. My evenings matter for many reasons. Long days on the road with all the people and scenery are certainly important and are probably the most interesting to read about. But a good night with no hassles sets me up for the next day. Remember my goal of "One day at a time?" In the perfect scenario, I am able to find reasonable accommodations along the route, or if not exactly on it, then close by will do. My bike rides, when I can travel much further quickly, have caused me to chase a perceived good deal on a motel for 4-5 miles. On foot, other than the mess I ran into in Franklin, I don't want to have to go much more than a mile. In the perfect world, food and water are both close by, and it only takes a few minutes to get what I need of both.

But the right motel, campground or even church, are the key to rest, planning and just general comfort for the evening. It also helps with reasonable success for the next day, too. The night at the Siler City Motor Lodge came close to meeting my standards for a perfect evening. As I recap that evening, I can't remember a single thing that wasn't just as it should be. I've mentioned before that I don't need or even want a real frilly room. A clean room with just the basics fits the bill for me. Some extra space is always a plus, as well as finding everything in working order. I hate a super dark room, especially if it is due to bulbs being burnt out. A refrigerator is most important, and a microwave not so much but still good to have. On hot days, being able to keep the water cold for the continual drinking of the evening helps with rehydrating, which is an almost daily issue. The shower, which is right near the top of the list, needs to have good pressure and late evening hot water. Often, as I have said before, I go to bed right after a good shower to cap off the day.

I like a firm bed but really don't care much about its size. Firm pillows are my favorite, too, maybe because I sleep best on my back with my head elevated. I've mentioned the importance of a good heater, but it is equally as important to have a working air conditioner on a hot day. I don't like to camp on a cold or hot night and get recharged quicker if I can rest at a reasonable temperature. Often, the first thing I do in a room is turn on the heater or A/C because most motels don't keep them running when no one is in the room. The heater helps me dry clothes that I wash out in the sink or shower, and the A/C helps with that, too.

Otherwise, I need good WiFi for submitting my stories

and also for planning purposes. My iPad tips me off right away on the quality of the WiFi, and chasing around on a cold night to find a better signal isn't fun. I often ask about the power of the WiFi when calling ahead but have found such information from the front desk person to be virtually useless. It's better to ask upon arrival and get a good location. No doubt the staff knows where the WiFi works best. My travels out west are often dependent on WiFi because cellphone signals can be spotty.

The only remaining condition for me when it comes to accommodations is that I appreciate a quiet room and will often ask for the "quietest room in the motel." Usually I get it, too, especially in the areas where travelers often pass through on a bike or on their own feet. Beware of a group of construction worker trucks all parked together on a pleasant evening! I learned long ago not to accept any room that borders a work crew, especially if they have been in the same place for several nights. I have stories to tell of late and frustrating nights when I've had to contend with outside music and loud voices.

Beyond that, I don't need much. Other extras probably won't get used, but I did appreciate the fireplace in the room at Highlands. Nice and comfortable chairs out front or out back of the room are a real plus too, especially if I can pick up WiFi there.

The restful overnight at the Siler City Motor Lodge ended, and I was up and going before dawn, about 5:45 a.m. I had seen the long sidewalk ahead the previous afternoon and hoped it would last through the other side of town. If it did, I would have no problem walking in the dark. I did pass the Day's Inn that I had called the previous evening and was glad that I still had the extra $35 in my wallet for future expenses.

The good sidewalk took me to the other side of town, where I found great road shoulders and steady traffic that didn't bother me a bit. I passed the last few stores in town and didn't think much of it, expecting more along the way toward Cary. In an area where U.S. 64 is considered a major road, how could there not be more stores? What I found were 20 miles without a single convenience store and plenty more rumble strips. Those dreaded things had returned, the kind that left me no room on the now narrow shoulder. I also found a long strip where the median was cabled in order to keep anyone from crossing over. Not only was there no scenery worth noting, I continued to encounter growing traffic and rumble strips! Without stores, no chances for conversation occurred. This was one of the toughest sections throughout the whole journey.

Hoping to gain a small edge by staying out of the grass, I crossed to face traffic again. Gaps in the cable came near creek bridges. My strategy to stay sane and make good time was to jump in the traffic lane as long as possible between traffic rushes. Realistically, I was on and off the pavement about equal amounts of time, but it was never boring. Drivers who went ahead and pulled over into the passing lane to allow me to stay on the pavement were again greatly appreciated.

I did see an alpaca farm and stopped to take some photos. Big dogs were guarding the alpacas but soon tired of barking at me. I don't think they were all that ferocious anyway. There was a huge logging operation too. Imagine several hours of nothing but dodging traffic and thinking that alpacas were a highlight!

After a morning that had been just a slog to get the miles behind me, things suddenly changed for the better. I went down a hill, crossed a river and the rumble strips stopped! My spirits lifted almost immediately. A no contact with people morning changed, too, as four cyclists passed by while I was climbing a hill. The last one circled back, asking, "So you are really running across the state?" We started an enjoyable conversation. Craig Mangum, an emergency room doctor at Wake Medical Center, wanted to know more about my journey and told me a little bit about himself. Craig was into fitness and had been an ER doctor for eight years. He was headed later to spend time with his son's scout troop, so we made a few pictures and off he went.

Just as Craig rode away, Jerry Womack and Carol Vaught stopped by. They live near Cary and had some interesting plans that coincided with my adventure. Jerry, originally from Spencer, had been following my story and grabbed Carol to come find me passing through the area. Both of them planned to drive to Manteo later and run my route in reverse all the way back to the Tennessee line west of Murphy. Jerry planned to stop by the Salisbury Post and pick up all the back issues they had with stories of my travels so they could read the highlights.

I had an unusual goal for the day. My distance goal was to reach the area near Jordan Lake, a huge recreational lake along U.S. 64. Even with a cold wind blowing, the sun glistened off the water to make the lake look very inviting. I did see one small craft that looked from the distance like a sailboat. Road construction in the area appeared to have the purpose of installing a new water pipe alongside it. The construction allowed me to have a lane to myself as I rode inside the long line of orange barrels.

On this Friday afternoon, I planned to leave the route again and head home for the weekend. Tim and William Deal came to pick me up in this construction area, and the stop went well. I had made 28 miles for the day, leaving the road in high spirits with only about a third of my across the state journey to go.

I had a longstanding commitment to work a 5K race in Mooresville on Saturday and a few other things I needed to do. My run/walk would resume on Monday morning, again with the assistance of Tim and William, who had offered to bring me back to the same spot. One big issue was that I had worn out the Altra Paradigm shoes that I had been wearing exclusively since the third day. Ralph Baker's Shoe Store at home, our local running shoe supplier, had arranged for a new pair of the same shoes. I was really looking forward to them as I expected running opportunities to improve once I passed through Cary and Raleigh and hopefully reached the flattest part of the state.

While my little collection of found coins was growing, I had been quite surprised to find out from his daughter that Ed Dupree used to do the same thing. He spent lots of time along the roads, running over 40,000 miles through all 100 counties in North Carolina. His daughter, Allison Adams, had already informed me that Ed's spirit was close by. The one quarter I found today looked worn enough to have been dropped by him as a young man. The difference between me and Ed when it came to the coins we found was that I had no idea how much mine totaled. Ed would have known about his down to the penny.

I was extremely fortunate to have Tim and William take me back to the same exact spot. Tim had picked me up at 4:30 a.m., and I was already excited and ready to go. This was definitely slated to be a long day. Both Deals are very interesting conversationalists and the time passed by quickly. I was dressed for more cold and watched the temperatures gradually fall throughout the trip. They dropped me off at 7:30 a.m. and sent me on my way with a wonderful prayer and plenty of photos to document the trip. I felt good, very good in fact, and the still hilly miles began to pass as I neared Cary. My shin was doing OK but by now

I expected that healing on the little aches and pains would not come until I was completely off the road for a month or more.

Gradually the day started to warm as the road swelled to six and sometimes eight lanes in Cary. U.S. 64 joined with U.S. 1, a road that I used for most of my 2014 Maine to Key West cycling adventure. That trip had included a serious car-versus-bicycle accident in Tequesta, Florida. It was one of the great stories of my life after being knocked off my bike toward traffic. Luckily I escaped without serious injury. U.S. 1 is a road that will forever hold part of my heart, just as U.S. 64 was becoming just as important to me.

U.S. 1 soon peeled off, and I was suddenly on Interstate 40/U.S. 64. Whenever this has happened in most western states while I was on a bicycle, I was just another vehicle and had "Share the Road" signs posted for my protection. But this time, with me being on foot, I didn't know what to expect. North Carolina interstates usually have large signs, especially near entrances that prohibit pedestrians, farm equipment, slow moving vehicles, etc. I didn't see any of these signs and still had a wide shoulder to use. Still, the uncertainty of this environment was slightly troubling. Patrick Smith had talked to a fellow officer at the Cary Police Department who had told him I would be fine and that runners use this area on occasion. Cary PD cars drove by regularly, and none of the officers stopped to say anything. If anybody had stopped me, I planned to plead ignorance because I actually felt that way. Nothing worked better than just putting one foot in front of the other and rolling the jogger forward. I tried not to worry but did expect something to happen soon. It did, but not like I expected.

I kept going through a major construction area that lasted for miles. Barrels were everywhere, often leaving me an even better protected place for safe passage. Speaking of those barrels, I saw a worker walking toward me and expected him to ask me to find another way through town. The exact opposite happened as he wanted to know all about my run and why I had decided to do it this way. Right away, he wanted to contribute to my expenses, and I declined to accept any money. This offer comes up quite often on my cycling adventures, and I have never accepted. On certain occasions, residents have bought me meals or chipped in on some expense, such as motel rooms, but I never want to just take their money. The worker kept after me, saying, "Could I at least give you $5 toward a meal? I know that you are probably eating a lot." Imagine how horrible I felt when he opened his wallet and only had $10, which he handed to me. I wanted to give it back but he was so happy to do it, I didn't have the heart to turn him down. The worker wouldn't give me his name or allow me to take a picture, but he did tell me that he wanted to walk a specific route of 100 miles from his hometown to the capital city of his state or country. I hate to admit that I didn't totally understand part of that information. This was very moving, and I will certainly always remember that he gave me his last $10.

I was now in Raleigh and didn't expect things to change so quickly. I was daydreaming along the route when I spotted a Raleigh Police Department car as it pulled over ahead of me. Officer E.H. Patton walked back toward me in a nonthreatening manner and read the sign on the baby jogger. I enjoyed telling him about my plans, and the whole conversation was very upbeat. Officer Patton told me that a motorist had called in that I was in the median but nothing was said about the "baby." Early in the conversation, I expected him to address me being on the interstate, but it was never mentioned. A friendly guy, Officer Patton said it was OK to take a picture of his car with the baby jogger and I did, but he didn't want to be in it.

About 20 minutes later, things took a strange turn. Another Raleigh Police Department car with the same color and logo made a fast appearance, quickly stopping in front of me. I described it afterwards as him sliding to a stop but he actually didn't. No black marks were left, but the stop was quite quick. Just as this happened, I noticed that another one had stopped behind me and hit his squawk siren. I jumped when I heard it, but remember immediately shaking my head. This was developing as a very odd day.

The officer in front walked toward me and said nothing while the one in the back kept his hand on the handle of his firearm, asking, "Sir, what are you doing?" He also asked to see my driver's license which seemed really odd. At that point, was a driver's license required to push a stroller along the road? And was I a big enough threat to require being stopped by two cars and essentially hemmed in? I told the officers that I had just been stopped 20 minutes before and they seemed surprised that I gave them the officer's name. The rear officer then said, "Did that officer check your license?" I said that he did not and that we had a very good talk about my journey across the state. The rear officer then told me that one of the cameras in a light tower along the way made me look like I was out on the interstate using a walker, one of those mobility improvers. I saw no resemblance even from a distance away.

When I mentioned that I was chronicling the whole story for our local newspaper, their demeanor changed quite a bit. Both broke out in a smile, and the front officer told me he had never heard of Manteo. The rear officer asked, "Will we be in tomorrow's story?" I told him that they would, to which he replied, "Just say that Officer Good Looking and Officer Bald stopped you." The rear officer, referring to himself as being good looking, laughed more than the "bald" officer did, and they both got in their cars, wishing me luck before they left. I was glad to be leaving Raleigh.

Before the end of the day, I had two more challenges. The traffic volume was huge, and I had to cross over four lanes of very fast traffic to stay on U.S. 64. This worried me more than most things did because the traffic was so fast that any perceived gap closed faster than I could sprint across the pavement. The road began to divide with a slight median in the middle, which was big enough for the stroller and me. After conjuring up enough courage, I took off and realized that the traffic was slowing for me until I made it across. I waved to all, and the excitement had passed. You can imagine that several immediate prayers were whispered just prior to the sprint, and once again, they were answered. I told a friend the other day that my prayers often can't wait for long-term answers. Yes, I am impatient more than not, but I am sure that God knows which ones to mull over and which ones to answer quickly. He has gotten it right every single time.

As time passed, I started to think about finding a place to spend the night. Several choices were within a few miles but only one caught my eye. I had about four miles to go, and the motel would be about two of those miles out of the way for the next day's journey. U.S. 64 was about to turn east and I had to continue on to another exit and go west briefly. Just as I approached the 64 exit, a car slid — literally slid this time to a stop against the guardrail — right in front of me with smoke and/or steam coming out of it. All three occupants jumped out of the car, leaped over that guardrail and ran screaming from the car. Several trucks stopped next and one of the drivers sprayed the car with a fire extin-guisher before the car driver asked him to go back and cut the engine off. The truck driver did that just as I walked past, knowing that the car occupants were in good hands.

I noticed that the front end of the car had lots of damage. There must have been an accident in traffic but they didn't need me.

I found the next exit quickly and asked Siri to help me find the motel, just as I confused her by walking up the wrong exit (actually the entrance for cars) because it was shorter than the correct entrance. I hope that made sense. Instead of being less than a mile to the motel, Siri suddenly upped the total to more than three miles and wanted me to make a U-turn. I checked the address on the motel and continued on, arriving just a little quicker at the Wake Inn, located just across from Wake Medical Center. My head was spinning from listening to hours of fast driving cars, much of it on concrete. Tire roar is much louder on concrete, and I hate hearing it. Finally, I had left behind that punishing sound for at least the evening.

The Wake Inn had another story of its own. I had called ahead and spoke to a desk clerk with limited English capability and later found out that he was the owner. On that call, I was transferred to his son, who spoke much better English and gave me a really good price for a location within Raleigh and especially one that was near a major hospital. The sign posted the same price and the motel itself looked really good, so I was happy with the choice.

As I attempted to check in, I was told that there were no rooms remaining at the special price. Neither were there any remaining downstairs rooms. Going upstairs with the stroller isn't a big deal. It's much less of a workout than taking a heavily loaded bike up a flight or two of steps. Of course, in certain situations, I can unhook the heavy bags and make a special trip down to get them. The benefit of an upstairs room is generally a quieter room with no sounds of footsteps above the ceiling.

Knowing that an upstairs room might be a better choice, I still asked to see the room first. I had not booked a room on the phone but the upcharge was only $4 for a double room. My first look at the proposed room took only a second for me to see that I was getting a very high quality and probably quiet room for a fantastic price. I raced back down and paid for it.

After 31 miles on the road, two police stops and the first miles in my very comfortable new Altra Paradigms, I was in a great room that didn't have a screaming truck in sight. I found an amazing sub shop next door and immediately ordered a large veggie calzone, perfect for replacing carbs and calories after a long day. Still missing water and some other snacks, I crossed over to the nearby Walgreens and loaded up. Long ago, I had learned that a weary traveler can eat pretty well out of a Walgreens and can certainly get by if a microwave is available. My room had everything I needed, and I was set for yet another restful evening. I would need it with the events of the next day about to unfold.

Some days are people days and some are scenery days. A few of the best days have plenty of both. Other than police officers, I had very few conversations on Tuesday, so I hoped for more on Wednesday. As I planned the Wednesday route on Tuesday night, I had a big dilemma. I couldn't make it to Rocky Mount in one day or at least didn't think I could because that distance was well over any daily mileage that I had completed so far. Finally, I went to bed to "sleep on it" and decide in the morning.

Up early again, as had happened nearly every day, I knew exactly how to get started with a short backtrack to U.S. 64. I jumped back on the same road that brought me to the Wake Inn's exit the previous afternoon, noticing road signs that included U.S. 64, U.S. 264, Bypass 495 and Interstate 87. That was a lot of roads, a ton of traffic and no stated issue with a guy who was probably considered a pedestrian. Traffic was heavy and loud, and I listened to my radio music in hopes of drowning out the roar. The morning was cold, and rain was expected later.

Still putting off my decision for road choice, I continued on U.S. 64 and U.S. 264 as the other roads eventually peeled off in other directions. After passing by Knightdale and arriving in Zebulon, the only town I know of with a minor league baseball team and no motels, it was decision time. I had to divert to Wilson and follow U.S. 264 for a long day or try for Rocky Mount and hope for an unlisted motel way before Rocky Mount. If I chose the Rocky Mount route and didn't find a motel, I would be way up in the night arriving there. Terrible rumble strips on U.S. 64 had persisted for several hours and pushed me into the wet grass, especially as the multi-lane road reverted to a side-by-side two lane road.

On that early portion, I was stopped yet again, this time by Wake County Deputy Sheriff Evans. A call had come in about my "baby," and it led to another enjoyable conversation with a quality officer just doing his job. Deputy Evans seemed more interested in my long journey and I enjoyed telling him about some of the other law enforcement stops, especially the two-car stop the day before.

Once the rain started in earnest, I noticed a vehicle up ahead with a trailer loaded with rolls of carpet. Kenny Flowers had stopped to check on his load and waited until I was passing him before he asked, "Do you need a ride?" I told Kenny that I was doing this because I wanted to and was probably headed to Wilson as the best option. He said, "That is where I am going, and you are welcome to ride along!" My answer was the same standard from before, "I have to do it all on my own two feet, but thanks for asking." Kenny was not the first to ask, "Why?"

Looking for any edge to stay on the most direct route which meant staying with U.S. 64, I called Nashville, Zebulon and Spring Hope to see about lodging with no success. Peter Asciutto, a longtime friend and owner of Vac and Dash running store in Albemarle, used to sell vacuum cleaners in the area and checked with a few of his sources. The final report from all sources uncovered no available lodging within that day's run/walk distance until Rocky Mount.

As I stopped on the exit to U.S. 264 and Wilson, I pondered what to do. I was about to put my map and phone back in my waterproof bag and push on to Wilson when I noticed a car had stopped ahead of me. The driver had her door open and was motioning toward me. Tia Hooker wanted to make sure I didn't need any help with directions or anything else. We had a nice talk and with her information, I confirmed that Wilson was the right choice. After quality visits with Kenny and Tia, I had no idea what would happen on the rest of the way to Wilson. The distance to Wilson was far enough away to realize that dark would be pushing hard if the clouds persisted at dusk. I told myself that I had no time to waste.

U.S. 264 was a much better road, and most of the time, I could keep at least two wheels on the pavement. Drizzling rain persisted but the cold had lessened somewhat. I noticed a car up ahead and thought it must be another law enforcement officer but it was odd that nobody was exiting as I approached. Only one of the officers had stayed in his car, and most had hopped out as soon as they stopped. Just as I started to pass by the car, I noticed the window being lowered by a lady sitting behind the wheel with tears in her eyes. Courtney Farmer works in the same area as the Wake Inn and had seen me early that morning heading east. She told me she had worried all day and vowed to find me after work. She had just been on the phone after riding around trying to locate me. I was thankful that there were such good people still left in the world and for getting to meet a lot of them. Courtney's effort was moving to me because she didn't know a thing about me, but she did realize that I needed to be safe by nightfall and set out to make sure I was. All I could do was explain why I was out in the bad weather and that my journey was much closer to the end than the beginning. But most of all, I wanted her to know that she had genuinely touched me. We shook hands, and she smiled.

As late evening drew nearer, I saw another woman pull over ahead of me and get out to walk toward me. Natalie Newcomb of Lucama had stopped to check on me, too, and offer a ride. I misunderstood her when she first spoke and nodded yes, so Natalie set about to find a way to haul the stroller in her car. After understanding what she was doing, I said, "No, I want to be doing this, and I have to do it on my own. I don't need a ride." By then, she had read my sign and understood. Natalie took time to make a selfie with me, but not until she had brushed her hair. We laughed and had a good time with that one. Natalie also made sure I knew where I was going. We both waved as she drove away.

Just a few minutes later, Roberto and Jose stopped to also offer me ride. These guys had just left work at the same grading company and asked "Why?" when I told them about crossing the state. No matter, they wished me luck and drove away with still more smiles.

Deputy Smith of Nash County pulled over next, but this time I had been accused of running away with a baby so he asked to see my ID. I complied and let him read my sign and see the bags and confirm that there was no baby. Deputy Smith said, "We just had to check it out. Sorry for the bother." I told him that I been stopped numerous times across the state and about half the time, it had to do with the "baby."

Just before dark and near my exit, Natalie came back to check on me again, thinking that I may not have understood her directions for the small group of motels. The cold had returned as the dark approached but the rain had stopped. I assured Natalie that I was on the right path and would be there shortly after dark with my safety lights flashing.

It was pitch dark when I was stopped for the last time by another motorist who had seen me early that morning, nearly 38 miles away. He had his family in the SUV, and I told them all what I was doing. I got a real boost when the kids expressed their amazement!

Just a little more than a mile away, I found the Microtel that offered a $44 price for the night. Remember that price as I will write more about that in the next chapter.

The counties of Rowan, Davie, Davidson, Randolph, Chatham, Johnston and soon to be Wilson were now also in my rear view mirror.

Before closing this day, I have trouble expressing what all

these caring people meant to me. I was a thin and bearded guy walking or running beside a very busy road on a cold and damp day. No one had to stop to see about me, but countless people did. Natalie and Courtney went way out of their way to make sure I would finish the day in a warm place. On no other day over my years of adventures across our great nation had I been touched in such a way. These people, black, white and Hispanic, generally cared about their fellow man. How could I be more blessed than to have received this day and these encounters? I truly do not know.

# CHAPTER 7

*The homestretch begins —*
*The weather finally improves*

· · · · · · · · · · · · · · · · · · · · · · · · · · · · · · · · · · · · · · · · · · · · · · · · · · · · · ·

W ith my late arrival on the outskirts of Wilson, I had two thoughts: finding some food and a warm motel in the small cluster near U.S. 64 that offered the only options for several miles. It was already dark and I had planning to do for Wednesday, the first full day off of U.S. 64. I had seen low prices offered in the area online but was wary that all of these motels seemed to be chains, and low prices such as $44 were hard to come by with that group.

Still I walked into the Microtel, a chain that I had never visited, and asked to get one of the $44 rooms offered on the flashing sign outside. The clerk didn't laugh at me, but she did look at me sideways. This was not a weekend night or holiday nor had I heard of any special events in the area. Still, the first words from her mouth were, "Oh, I sold all of those rooms early this afternoon. I have a room for $80 a night, but I only have one more left." I had already seen two other motels with similar signs outside either touting ridiculously low prices or a specific price in the same range. I knew it was a racket to get people to stop in and inquire, from where the hook could be set. My own concern was that I was being hooked but were there other options? I thanked her and started to walk out to check on one of the other places. With another car driving up to the entry, I made a quick deduction and turned around to tell her I would take the room.

The driver of that other car did come in and ask the same thing that I had about the $44 room. This was a real test, I thought, because if she told him that she had more rooms at the same price as I had just committed to, then there was some dishonesty going on. To her credit, the clerk who I think was also the manager, said, "I am so sorry. This man just got the last room." She didn't tell him how much that $44 room really cost but he left happily thinking he could find a good deal at one of the other places. Then things started improving. Since I wasn't familiar with Microtel, I asked about breakfast. She said, "Yes, we have breakfast and it starts tomorrow at 5:30 a.m." I was amazed because very few motels have breakfast anymore, and those that do start at 6 or 7 a.m.

By this time, I was starving, even though I had some things in my bag and had just stopped at the McDonald's next door. What made me smile was the clerk's offer, "I have fresh baked cookies right here," she said, adding "Take as many as you want because they have been out for an hour." I didn't care if they had been out for two to three days, I grabbed a big handful and started on the first one as I walked the stroller up the stairs to my room. Once inside, I assessed the room for the price and counted it as just OK. The room was small, the TV was small and the water pressure wasn't great. The heater, however, was wonderful, and there was a huge picture window with a cushioned bench along it. All in all, though, some of the amenities were good and some not so good. I was off the road and finally warm and would soon no longer be hungry. I felt just fine about things.

As I ate and worked on my story, I kept glancing at the maps trying to figure out how I might reconnect with 64 and not lose much ground. The answer and directions became apparent, and I settled into finishing the story and photos and submitting them. On this unusual day, I couldn't remember any scenery that mattered. But I met plenty of good people, which was always high on my list. I used the hot shower for what it was worth, can't remember turning on the TV, and went straight to bed but not before tallying the $0.45 in coins found for the day. I had plenty for which to be thankful.

Thinking I had a handle on piecing together a very rural route through the country back to Tarboro, I was going to be successful at bypassing Rocky Mount, the largest town left on U.S. 64. I was ready for small towns, less traffic and few large and loud trucks. My goal upon rising was to check out the breakfast and as the clerk said last night, "Take plenty of the prepackaged stuff for eating later." I thought to make up a little of the higher cost of the room by leaving with some good carbs for energy in my bag as I headed toward Tarboro. Individually packaged muffins were high on my list.

What I found in the breakfast room was a first. Every single table and chair was filled with folks dressed in jackets and shirts from a solar panel company. They were loud and bordering on obnoxious for 5:30 a.m., so I just grabbed one of the few remaining bagels and an orange juice and left them to their early morning food stuffing. I went back to the room and packed the stroller, rolled it down the stairs and greeted one of my first early mornings while wearing shorts.

Not sure of what was to be found on a succession of rural roads, I took time within the first mile to load up my bags for the day at the first store I found. I headed east right into the sunrise, my favorite all-time direction. I had the feeling that today would be alright. The folks in the convenience store were nice, my music was good, and by nightfall, I would have less than 150 miles remaining to reach the Atlantic Ocean. The weather was finally mild, and I doubted that I would hear a rush of traffic at any time during this day.

Passing through the outskirts of Wilson and continuing east could not have been easier. My direction also included a long angle toward the north with a route that had been planned well, having added 10 additional miles last night to find a room. Since I missed most of Wilson, I was glad to enter the small town of Elm City, which was brand new to me. I saw Kester Mitchell standing in his yard and watching me as I neared his side of town. Since he kept watching me, I decided to initiate a conversation. As we talked, our discussion covered cycling, walking and my choice of the route to Tarboro. Kester agreed with the route I had chosen and told me where to expect to make the first turn. He also told me about the two convenience stores in town. I vowed to hit the last one just in case there were few supply points ahead.

As I walked through the town, I noticed lots of historical looking homes and buildings. Elm City didn't look to be thriving, but it wasn't dying either. I bought some more snacks and checked to make sure my water was still good. I did find out that Elm City was historically significant for a 1964 racial uprising when black and white teens were working together to renovate a popular church. It seems some of the other locals didn't like the integrated work, causing enough unrest for National Guard troops to be directed to Elm City by then North Carolina Governor Terry Sanford. A group of integrated adults finished the job under protection of the troops.

As the day continued to warm, I shed my jacket and was dressed as lightly as I had been so far on this long adventure. There was lots of cropland between Elm City and Tarboro, but not much else. Agricultural lime was being spread on several fields, and a few tractors drove about but with nothing else really of note.

There were some houses and the fine weather had brought more than a few homeowners out to work in their yards. I would have been doing the same if I had been at home most likely after so many cold, wet and windy days breaking for a day that finally felt like spring. I saw James Mullins near the road painting his driveway fence rails white, and as we both turned to look at each other, I could see a conversation coming. James was so excited that I was out on his road and had been watching me approach from a long way off. He said, "I can't believe that somebody crossing the state on foot is coming by here. We talked some about Salisbury and what to expect on the way to Tarboro. James was also a cyclist and told me about upcoming road shoulders and where to watch for traffic.

James called his wife, Beatrice, over, and we all talked some more before I decided to get a picture. James told me their address was Pinetops but added that no towns were close by. I hated to say good-bye, but wanted to be off the road by much earlier than I had the previous night.

On the way to Tarboro, the road kept shrinking and growing shoulders. A good cyclist could have spent the whole time going back and forth across the road finding the best shoulder. I did see a restored 1854 doctor's office from an early plantation. The area had that plantation feeling with plenty of giant fields and not many homes except for a few which were quite stately and large.

Traffic was probably the heaviest I had encountered on this day as I made the last few miles into Tarboro but was still nothing of concern. I did cross over U.S. 64 and noticed right away that the highway had rumble strips and no significant shoulders at its edge. In addition, U.S. 64 was a four-lane highway here, with two on each side, and I knew that I would not leave the famous road again until I reached the ocean.

After 33 miles, I hit the jackpot again when I saw the Budget Inn, which I had called the previous night, and a Waffle House just across the road. Isn't it amazing how simple things can cause great joy? A large convenience store sat in between, leaving me sure that I would have everything I needed within a short walk. Before going to the motel, I stopped and bought the proverbial waffle, omelet and hash browns. The motel looked good from a distance, and the cars there seemed fine, too. I had hoped for the best and found it. The priced quoted was the one I got, and the owner was very pleasant. Another upstairs room which only cost me $49 was first class and made for a contented evening. I did visit the convenience store for more water, having run low again, and a few snacks for later, but my feet stayed up most of the time that evening. All in all, I was riding a hot streak on finding reasonable motels and food close by on this trip. The days were counting down, and I calculated that I had passed the 500-mile mark for the journey so far. With roughly 145 miles to go, Williamston and Plymouth would be coming up next.

The first warm day of the trip made me crave ice cream. I planned to find some soon, possibly using the dime I had found today. It was time for an early turn-in so I could get up refreshed and attack the rumble strips on Thursday morning.

Rested and pleased with my night at the Budget Inn, I was on the road again before daylight with red lights flashing. U.S. 64 was very close, just a long golf shot from the motel, and I started the day by loading up on water at the convenience store. I was taking no more chances after running low too often. The baby jogger and I again went the wrong way into the exit, expecting to battle the rumble strips just as I had two days before. I planned to take advantage of open gaps and use the pavement before getting back off again.

Another warm day was coming with temperatures already in the 50s as dawn broke and I realized that the long pants wouldn't be used again as the Atlantic Ocean began to draw nearer. Of course, my prayers that morning had addressed the rumble strips, so it really shouldn't have been any surprise at all that the shoulder widened to interstate width just about a mile into the day's journey. The rumble strips remained, but I hardly noticed them from several feet away. I planned to "rumble" on, but my mind knew that a change back could come at any time.

Luckily, nothing about the shoulders or rumble strips did change that day on the 32 miles to Williamston. The mileage was gradually creeping up each day on average, and my secret goal of "a marathon a day" was within reach. If I could up my average to at least 26.2 miles a day, I would be totally happy.

Speaking of happy, the road was wonderful. I enjoyed listening to my music and looking at the scenery with no worries at all. The only conversation I had all morning was with Danny Jones of Goldsboro, who was part of a landscape crew working along U.S. 64. Danny was eager to tell me about the work they were doing along the road, mostly at overpasses and intersections. Plantings and large decorative rocks were installed using ground fabric, all of which interested me because of the many years I had spent in horticulture distribution.

There weren't any other interactions during my day on the road, but things sure changed when I got to town. My exit off U.S. 64 was No. 214, and it pointed me toward the Ross Motel. Almost as soon as I made the turn, I found a wallet. It was under the overpass of 64 and had just missed landing in some standing water. The wallet didn't have any cash in it, but did have an ID, credit card and some other information. I couldn't find a phone number, so I dropped it in my handlebar bag to be dealt with later. I was ready to find the motel, another one that quoted a good price when

I called. Unfortunately, that call would serve as a reminder that price wasn't everything.

I saw a sheriff's car at a mechanic shop and asked if there was an officer nearby with hopes of giving him the wallet. It was funny to me that I was looking for law enforcement when they had been looking for me so often on this trip. No officer was close by so I continued on.

Arriving at the motel, I stopped by the office and told the guy at the desk that I had just called. The clerk gave me a room at what he said was the lowest price, but I had to pay cash for a key deposit. I told him that this hadn't happened to me in a long time and that I would be leaving very early. As if in slow motion, he processed my room request, telling me that the office was always open and I could get the key refund at any time.

I went to the room and found that there was no chair or remote. I went back to the office and asked for both, or the possibility of being moved to another room. The clerk said, "I can't move you to another room. There is no chair in the non-smoking rooms, and I am sorry about there being no remote." I thought that move, too, was rather odd because I was yet to dirty up anything in the room. He called the owner, who just happened to be in the next room because I could hear him talking. The clerk told the owner that I wanted a chair and a remote, and quickly the owner and his son appeared. The son grabbed an extra remote and tried it on the TV in the lobby to make sure it worked. The owner went to the room ahead of me and looked for a chair and remote in the room even though I could hardly understand what he was saying. A chair was sitting outside a room a few doors down, and he asked if that chair would work. I told him yes, as he tried to get the remote and the TV to work. It wouldn't, so he went in another room and got one that did work.

Later, I went back to the office, and the desk clerk told me that this was just his second day on the job and that he was truly sorry. He also stated that usually he could not understand what the owner wanted. Had they not worked it out or moved me to another room, I was ready to call the Williamston Police Department about more than just the wallet.

With all of this finally settled, I decided to go ahead and search for food. In this location, I had a Dairy Queen several blocks away and a Walmart across the road. The pull for the ice cream won easily against the pull of the grocery store food. Just as always, I was almost immediately refreshed with the ice cream.

Back at the room, I called the police department about the wallet, and a car arrived within five minutes. I gave the officer a card and thought of asking if he had heard of me, but didn't push my luck. I showed him the wallet and told him how I had found it, and he asked me a few other questions about the exact location. I did tell him why I was there and that I had spotted it when coming off U.S. 64. He sat in his car outside my room for about 10 minutes and then left. I hoped the desk clerk and owner wondered about why he was there.

Nothing else unusual happened during the evening. I already knew that Williamston was the home of the famous baseball brothers, Gaylord and Jim Perry. Gaylord was rumored to possess one of the best spitballs of the modern era of baseball. Williamston, just as Elm City, was also the center of significant racial unrest. In 1963, civil rights activists protested at City Hall for 29 consecutive days amid a significant era of Ku Klux Klan activity. Williamston is also on the Roanoke River.

My total of money found on this day was $0.85, better than most days, and I planned to give it to my church. Rodney Phillips, as financial advocate for the First Baptist Church in China Grove, had proposed that I donate all found money to the church. Of course, I agreed.

After all the trouble getting in it, the motel room was quiet and very adequate except for one more thing. About 1 a.m., the smoke alarm started chirping about once every five minutes. Though it was not too loud at first, I could no longer ignore it after 20 minutes or so. I grabbed my one chair and climbed up, took the smoke alarm apart and pulled out the battery. Finally, there was silence! This was the only warm night so far, and I ran the air conditioning unit briefly, a first for this trip. The days continued to wind down and my sights were set on Plymouth, a town with which I was already familiar. Rain was in the forecast but it looked as if I had survived the last of the cold.

I stopped by the motel office to get my $5 key deposit at 6:30 a.m., and no one was in the office. I kept ringing the buzzer while another motel guest joined me. I rang until a woman got up and brought us our $5 bills. She said nothing, just took the keys and handed back the money. I said, "Thank you!" and hit the road, headed toward a big convenience store that doubled as a truck stop in order to reload my bags. I didn't expect to find any stores or towns until I reached Plymouth.

It was a beautiful and mild morning with some clouds already out, just the kind that make for a colorful sunrise on the right day. U.S. 64 started off just as I left it yesterday, wide and with a big shoulder. Traffic was extremely light on this early Friday morning.

When U.S. 64 turned east toward Plymouth, the road dropped down to a very limited shoulder. The skies were cloudy, and the terrain was almost flat by this time, but I still had to leave the road on occasion as trucks passed. More and more logging trucks were on the road, even though I realized that empty ones were coming toward me and full ones were on the other side going east.

My body was looking forward to a shorter day, a total distance of 23 miles. I wanted to ice one foot and the same shin if possible and put those feet up for a few hours. A nap would be nice, too, and some serious planning would be required for the last two days of running and walking. My mind was strong and ready, but my body was in need of a little rest.

On that cloudy morning, I noticed a man and his dog waiting for me. William "Dukey" Connell, who had his dog, Saint, with him asked about my trip after reading my sign. I am not sure that Saint read it but he was hopping around and seemed a little excited. Besides what I told Mr. Connell, he had plenty of interesting things to say. Mr. Connell loved riding bikes, but doesn't like the fat tire bikes of today because they require more effort. He also prefers the single-speed bikes. Mr. Connell told me about a box that was delivered to town about 10 years ago from Plymouth, Massachusetts to Plymouth, N.C., by bicycle. Mr. Connell said, "Yep, that guy rode his bike down here, dropped off the package and camped for the night. Then, he headed back the next day." I promised to mail a copy of the Salisbury Post for that day's report and a book, and I will certainly honor that promise. As interesting as Mr. Connell was to talk to, I had to go.

Around Jamesville, the logging trucks took over the road. The road shoulder was just barely wide enough for two wheels, so it made for a tight fit with the trucks. On a couple of occasions, I had to pull my elbows in tight, and at least once, a truck got way too close.

Just on the west side of Plymouth, the pine log trucks turned left and the hardwood ones kept going. I stopped at a convenience store and grabbed some food because I already knew that the Sportsman's Inn didn't have any stores nearby. At the very nice motel, I quickly got my room and sat in a chair outside, since WiFi was strongest there. It was fun to see those logging trucks going by, but this time a more comfortable 120 feet away.

The road money pickup had yielded only $0.35 today, partly because the shoulder had been so small for most of the day. While walking on the tight shoulder, I made a conscious effort to acknowledge all the drivers who gave me room instead of pushing me into the grass. I was enjoying sitting in an outside chair when a very nice pickup pulled in a couple of doors down. The driver got out and asked if I lived there. I, of course, told him that I did not and was only a couple of days away from reaching the coast on my adventure. "Will you be here later?" the driver asked, adding "I will donate to that." He went to his room and later left with a well-dressed woman who arrived in another car. I never saw that donation or either of them again about that matter.

I had been to Plymouth in 2014 on my Atlantic Coast cycling adventure and again in 2017 on my Outer Banks cycling trip. Both times had been fun and gone well. I was able to explore lots of the town's amazing Civil War history. The last Confederate victory in North Carolina had been fought in the downtown area, and the Confederate ironclad CSS Albemarle sank while moored on the Roanoke River, located in the same area. This time, on my feet and at a much slower pace, I had decided not to explore again.

The motel was very quiet, and I got the rest I needed. Only two days remained if I could stay on track to end my long journey on Easter Sunday. Expecting light traffic, I headed east with just a glint of a brightening eastern horizon. Once again, I needed to load up on supplies due to the uncertainty of sources later in the day. One particularly busy convenience store drew my attention. Once inside, I found that the grill was busy, but I was not particularly hungry so I didn't get any egg and cheese biscuits. My purchases included snacks and water, but I also needed batteries. When I couldn't find them, I asked the clerk who was very gracious to come out from behind the counter and actually grab them for me. The clerk slipped an Easter chocolate in my bag along with a copy of John 3:16. I found that very cool and thought it was a great way to start the day.

Familiar with downtown Plymouth, I passed through while recognizing a few sights from the past trip. I encountered four miles of curbing right next to the road, which could be a real obstacle to jump quickly if the need arose. But on this Saturday morning, the traffic didn't cause me a single worry, and I used the curbing to find a little extra change along the road. Most of that day's total of $0.95 cents was found along that four-mile stretch.

Once I left town, the curbing disappeared, and the rumble strips returned. They did not cause much of a problem as I was able to stay on the pavement most of the time.

Scenery highlights were few and far between with only one very large grain elevator and some working farm equipment worth special attention. I did see one homeowner burning a huge fire in his backyard during high westerly winds, raising quite a bit of smoke.

As I neared Columbia, I thought about how few conversation opportunities I had so far that day. My goal was to reach the Dalton House Motel, the only lodging in the area. In fact, just finding a listing for the Dalton House was hard. Only Google Assistant had it, and I had called the previous evening to check on a room. By then, my plan seemed fairly final for a long day to Columbia and an even longer day to the ocean. I needed a good night's sleep and hoped the Dalton House would be better than camping. WiFi was important because cellphone signals were poor in the area.

Once I was just inside the town limits, I realized that the Dalton House was very close, and in fact, I would have to make a quick reverse in direction on N.C. 94 to see the motel. I was immediately concerned that only one store was close by, and it was a small, yet busy convenience store. I noticed a driver who had just bought gas looking at me so I stopped to ask him what to expect. He said, "Yes, the motel is right there and this is the only store. The others are more than a mile away in the main part of town. You can get what you want to eat right here, but they will close at 6 p.m."

All that seemed OK, but I did not expect the upcoming entertainment when I went through the door. Only Ariel

Basnight, working the food and deli counter, and Buddy Davenport, not sure if he was an employee or a customer, were inside. I told Ariel that I was staying at the Dalton House and needed to get some food. Her menu was posted on the wall and I ordered, then looked for some snacks in the small offerings on the shelves.

Then it got to be fun. Another two customers came in that had seen my sign on the stroller. The conversation got around quickly to what I should expect on an Easter Sunday run to the coast. Things got interesting as the store crew told me about alligators and bears ahead. Alligators had been seen crossing the road, and bears were also common, especially when I passed through a wildlife refuge. One comment hit home: "Oh, I bet you will see a bear."

A local woman named Kay Grayson was called "The Bear Lady" and lived in a ramshackle trailer without power deep in the wilderness. Supposedly Grayson, a former Las Vegas showgirl, lived only to coexist with the bears and even alligators. She enjoyed feeding them and worked at a barbecue joint just to get the leavings that they loved. One day, she was found dead, possibly done in by the bears that she had fed for 28 years. The locals in the store didn't think the bears did it so I couldn't wait to look up some information about Grayson online. There was certainly plenty available. Everyone in the store seemed to have known her well.

Edgecomb, Martin, Washington and soon to be Tyrrell counties were now complete. Only Dare remained.

I had spent most of the day thinking about how to approach my last day on the road. Now I had at least a little concern about crossing through this bear and alligator area. I already knew that nothing about this store conversation would change a thing, but I would hustle through this area and keep my eyes open, especially in the early morning darkness. The last day's journey was just ahead!

# CHAPTER 8

*The most amazing day on the way to the sea —*
*Overtaken by emotion*

. . . . . . . . . . . . . . . . . . . . . . . . . . . . . . . . . . . . . . . . . . . . . . . . . . .

F ew days stand out on my adventures as much as this
one did. My evening was full of thoughts about how to
prepare for possibly the longest day of my journey with
many questionable variables. My goal of making it to Columbia was accomplished, technically anyway. I was in the
city limits but on the western side of the actual downtown.
My home for the evening was the Dalton House Motel,
which wasn't at all like a typical motel. Most of the motel
had already transitioned to apartments.

After calling the owner and learning how to get into my
room, I found a very large and nice room that looked as if it
had been recently remodeled. My goal for the evening had
been to get my story submitted and find the Final Four basketball game between Loyola of Chicago and Michigan on
TV. I quickly went to work on the day's story, but couldn't
keep my mind off the comments of the folks at the Short
Stop convenience store. I planned to research that information later in the evening.

I listened to the evening news in the background and realized that the game was being shown on WTBS instead of CBS and quickly tried to find it on the TV. The channels were very limited, and TBS was not one of the available ones so I would not get to see the game after all, which was a big disappointment for me. I already knew that this was the only motel in town or even close to it, and it was going to be chilly overnight. I had to be happy with being inside, but this scenario reminded me of previous disappointment on an evening during the last summer's long-distance bike ride from Washington to Wisconsin. One of my best friends from home had died unexpectedly that day. All I wanted to do was find the motel and some food after a long day, get my story in and watch a Yankees game quietly. The only motel in that town was very nice but their long list of channels did not include ESPN. To be more exact, it did include ESPN but the motel did not receive a signal for it. I couldn't believe this, and just as on this evening, I felt like my key to a nice evening had been taken away. Turns out that just the same as that earlier time, my team lost, which softened the blow a bit. It is way more fun to see them win.

While checking the score on my phone, I finished and submitted my story and photos for the day and realized that the WiFi was weaker than what I had hoped. I walked around the motel on an already chilly evening and finally got most of my submissions to transmit. I got the last one to go while back in the room.

With that, and no game to watch, I set about planning for what would be the longest and hopefully the last day of my journey across North Carolina. I checked various sources and found that the expected mileage should be between 41 and 42 miles to Jennette's Pier and only about four miles shorter to stop in Manteo. There was no reason to stop in Manteo with the final destination being that close. I decided to wave as I passed by.

The other concerns that weighed on my mind came from the various conversations earlier that afternoon at the Short Stop. I could tell from the map that U.S. 64 was going to downsize and that there were no towns between Columbia and Manteo. Supply points would be limited if there were any at all, and I was concerned because my food and water supplies were very low, especially for what might be the longest distance of the whole journey. That's not factoring in any businesses that might be closed for the Easter Sunday holiday.

I also recalled their comments about the bears and alligators that had been seen in the area. Knowing that I had no choice but to walk or run through there, I immediately thought of leaving very early. I planned to meet at least one friend at the pier and expected that there might be more. It would be very uncool to arrive in the dark and miss out on making the best photos. "But just how big was the bear and alligator threat?" I wondered. "Could I leave as early as 5 a.m. and get a jump on the distance and possibly the worst of the vacation traffic?" The one particular comment I remembered from the conversation at the Short Stop was, "Oh, I bet you will see a bear." Often, I had traveled in bear areas on my bike rides and had been warned about carrying food with me.

So, the bottom line was, "Should I leave really early and travel through the main part of Columbia too soon for any convenience store that might be opening on Easter with a goal of getting an early start? Or would I set myself up for a possible wild animal encounter in the dark, especially by having food with me?"

I needed the food but I wanted to make especially good time on this last day. I set the alarm on my phone for 4 a.m. and went to bed. As usual, I had no trouble sleeping to start with but awakened for a bathroom trip at about 2:30 a.m. No more sleep came as my mind overloaded, so my feet hit the floor at 3:25 a.m. ready to get packed to leave. By 4 a.m. and after some special prayers, the baby jogger and I hit the road. Just before leaving, I made a photo of the three packs of crackers and small pack of peanut butter cookies that constituted my food supply and filled an empty bottle with water from the bathroom tap. I had a couple more full water bottles.

The morning was brightened by a nearly full moon, and there was no wind. An eerie quiet and a light fog were part of the setting. I was immediately overcome with excitement for the day and all that it could include. This day could be one of my most rewarding and exciting ever. By getting quickly on N.C. 94, I walked toward the Short Stop that was in fact not yet open. A plastic bag was in the road as I walked by thinking briefly that maybe I should check it for contents just in case it had some edible food. A coyote raced across the road, making me wonder if this was a sign of things to come.

Back on U.S. 64, I tried to run a little bit and found that my shin issue was going to limit early running. I settled back into walking and headed toward the Scuppernong River and entry into the actual downtown area of Columbia. The historical town looked interesting in the dark and made me vow to return when I could see more of it in the daylight.

The third convenience store I passed was preparing to open at just before 5 a.m. with two workers inside. The sign on the door of the Eagle Mart said it would open at 5:30 a.m. but I was glad to see it happen much sooner. I had secretly hoped that none of the stores would be open just to see if doing 40 plus miles would be possible on just the crackers and cookies that I had. Realistically, this wasn't a good idea, and I waited for about five minutes until Kathy Webb opened the door and welcomed me and another lady customer into the store. Two very fresh egg and cheese biscuits were my first must-have items, and I then grabbed a few pastries and a large four-pack of Reese's Cups. I topped off my supply needs with another large bottle of water. I hit the road again after Judy assured me that there were no other stores along the route until Manteo.

The east side of Columbia had another store preparing to open and one more being built, but I didn't need to stop again. A meager sidewalk played out, and I headed toward the eastern sky with hopes that it would soon begin to brighten. As I left town, a white SUV drove by multiple times very slowly. This seemed very odd with few other vehicles on the road. A narrow road with no shoulder presented itself and loomed as a problem if the traffic increased.

Although I couldn't tell much about what was alongside the road, I could see that a lot of water was reflected. The road was very straight toward the east and appeared to be heavily wooded. Perfect for bears and alligators! I pushed on and saw the sky begin to brighten slightly as I listened to hymns on the radio. Brilliant colors began to appear as the prospect of a spectacular Easter morning sunrise loomed. I kept pushing toward a gap in the tree line that lay ahead hoping it might offer a clear view of the ever-nearing sunrise. Just as the big ball was about to break the horizon, the road turned in a more southern direction and my view of the actual sunrise was blocked by a densely wooded section. By mid-morning, I had reached the Alligator River and the Intracoastal Waterway. Most surprising at this point was a genuine lighthouse beside the river and a small convenience store that was open. As someone who loves lighthouses, I took some photos but rolled on past the convenience store.

The Lindsay Warren Bridge spanned the river and waterway and gave me just enough room for the baby jogger while facing moderate traffic. A drawbridge at the midway point was not being used although an operator was available. The long bridge was surrounded by spectacular scenery, and the experience was a pleasant break from the early morning, two-lane road with no shoulder. Wind was not an issue on this long bridge as it often is.

On the other side was the Wildlife Refuge, where the possibilities of bear and alligators increased. By now, traffic was quite a bit heavier, and with just one lane on each side, cars seemed to run in spurts as slower ones held up others. I stopped to eat the last of my breakfast biscuits, although I didn't think the alligators and bears were going to take a chance on me with so much traffic.

Up to this point, I had been singing along just about all morning with the hymns on the radio. Some of my singing had been really loud, but no one seemed to care. If they had, I still would have kept doing it anyway. Those songs had moved me, just as much as the beautiful developing morning and the fact that I felt great. While no thoughts ever entered my mind about fear, I began to think the biggest possibility of a serious animal encounter had passed.

Some of the more familiar hymns evoked tears, although this hadn't happened often on the trip. The day seemed to be heading toward an emotional conclusion as I wondered what Ed thought of the end nearing. I ate small food snacks often and made sure to keep drinking water as the day began to warm. A few cars waved or blew their horns lightly while none seemed perturbed that I was trying to push the stroller along the edge of the road.

Mann's Harbor was the first sort of town that I would find. Just a few miles west of there, the narrow U.S. 64 ended and a wonderful wide and freshly paved shoulder became my place of safety. Then something miraculous began to happen. I was totally worn out as the last 10 miles of the day loomed. My legs were dead, and the shin splint issue that had lingered since day three of the journey reared up again early that same morning.

Where my legs seemed done, I found new strength, and suddenly a surge of energy to run. Not fast, but I was running again even though I faced some uphills on the bridges and a front quartering wind. I remember running better than I had since Day 2 of this adventure and even pumping my arms because I could do it. I believe the power had to come from two sources. My God was helping me to the finish, having been with me through the suffering. I also remember thinking that Ed Dupree must be right there, too, gently with a hand on my shoulder helping me forward.

I'm sure this last homestretch was as much for him as it was for me. The miles clicked by faster than at any time that day, and the view from the bridges showed me that the ocean was just a few miles away.

I passed by the turnoff for the town of Manteo, no longer

needing to stop there. I was headed to the ocean, and the tears flowed again. Very few other athletic adventures had elicited the emotion of this day. Years before, in late 1980, I had broken three hours on my second marathon after falling apart in my first. The tears flowed as I neared that finish. My cross-country ride in 2013 included a route that let me stop by my farm before heading to the ocean in South Carolina. As soon as I turned onto Weaver Road where my farm is located, the tears began to spill. In none of these cases, neither could I stop them nor did I want to. I have participated in thousands of athletic events of different sorts and only three times have my emotions overwhelmed me. Today was the third of those days.

Drivers of the cars and trucks had started to wave and blow their horns with increasing frequency once I turned onto the better road. I didn't know why they were doing it but the interest from other people served as a big boost. I had continued to listen to the radio and upon hearing "Country Roads" by John Denver, I began to sing at the top of my lungs and pump my fists again. Tears flowed once more for what would be the last time. "Take me home, country roads" seemed so appropriate for the time. I couldn't believe that I could still find the strength to push that baby jogger up the hill and into the wind.

A friend from Corolla, Meghan Agresto, planned to meet me at the pier at our pre-arranged time of 6 p.m. I didn't count on the extra energy that God and Ed were providing so with just two miles to go, I was going to finish early. I sent Meghan a text, and found that she and her sons were still 19 minutes away so I pulled off the road to change into a different shirt, the Salisbury Rowan Runners club shirt. I took time to clean up a little bit and take a bathroom break. During the process, I snagged my leg on some briars and started bleeding. Just as I was about to head for the pier, Durham Merrell from Salisbury pulled over ahead of me. He was going fishing and had known that I would be on the road about this time. We had a nice talk, and I asked if he was going to the pier. Durham said he was headed on down to Avon but just wanted to stop to say hi and encourage me. He would be the last of the dozens of drivers who stopped along the way during my trip across North Carolina.

I received a text that Meghan and her sons, Paolo and Benicio, were in place so I ran on. Meghan and I had met at the Currituck Lighthouse that she manages this past November and have stayed in touch ever since. I crossed through an intersection past the end of U.S. 64, turned onto N.C. 12 and headed to the pier. My last steps for this adventure were being played out as I spotted Meghan. She took photos as my run/walk across North Carolina came to an end on a glorious late afternoon in the Whalebone section of Nags Head. A hug from Meghan and handshakes from Paolo and Benicio felt good as the long journey came to an end.

More of Meghan's friends showed up as we made more

photos, including those of my first-ever front wheel dipping of the baby jogger. The weather was perfect on the afternoon of an Easter day that I will never forget. The realization of the end of such a physically challenging and rewarding journey was difficult.

With that, I headed for the historic Sea Foam Motel, located less than a quarter mile away, and the tired legs had no trouble with the final cool down as I ran easily. One guy walking his dog even stopped me to ask about my run across the state, and of course, he was amazed. No more than me.

I checked into the oceanfront room and soon headed for dinner with Meghan and her friends. Later that evening, I submitted my story to the Post and realized that absolutely no planning was required for the next day. All I really needed to do was take it easy, walk on the beach and catch up on messages from friends at home and those I had met along the way.

A beautiful day dawned on Monday, April 2. The morning was perfect for a walk on the beach. My legs were tired but the beautiful weather made them work better than they would have otherwise. Plenty of communication and a few more photos highlighted the rest of the morning and early afternoon until a cold northwest wind began to pummel the ocean and anyone outside as the temperature dropped close to 30 degrees during the afternoon.

I picked up a rental car provided by another adventurer, ate a good and healthy dinner after a trip to the grocery store, and settled in to watch the national championship college basketball game between Villanova and Michigan. I was so tired that I could only stay awake for less than half of it.

After a restful evening, I headed for home along much of the same route used over the last few weeks. It was a very pleasant and enjoyable journey that ended in Salisbury, where I dropped off the rental car, enjoyed lunch at IHOP and then headed back home to the farm.

Another memorable adventure was truly complete!

# ANOTHER ADVENTURE

*Cycling ten days along the N.C. coast*

B ack in 2013, I finished my first long-distance bike ride. That one started in Astoria, Oregon, and ended at Myrtle Beach, S.C. At the end of it, just a few days later in fact, the idea of cycling the Outer Banks came up and I loved the thought of it. On Nov. 10, 2017, this adventure became a reality. Here is a bonus recap of that adventure. It ties in nicely to my run/walk across North Carolina as many of the same places are mentioned. The two journeys were just four months apart. I hope you enjoy riding along, not running or walking, yet again.

Just the day before on Nov. 9, I drove down to Morehead City and left my truck there until I could return days later with much more knowledge of our coastal state. Many of the towns on the itinerary were new to me while I had made brief visits to a few of them on a previous cycling ride. These included towns like Havelock, Arapahoe, Aurora, Belhaven, Washington, Edenton and Elizabeth City.

I remember stopping in Elizabeth City on my Atlantic

Coast ride in 2013 looking for ice cream and a bike shop. I found the ice cream. Of course, I will continue looking for my favorite pineapple milkshake at any of the Dairy Queens still open in the late fall.

Near the Virginia line, I plan to cross over to the Outer Banks and get a closeup look at towns like Duck, Corolla, Kill Devil Hills, Manteo, Rodanthe, Hatteras, and Ocracoke on the way back to Morehead City. Multiple ferry rides and plenty of ocean views sound exciting to me as I hope for favorable winds. What I was really looking forward to was meeting more wonderful people and enjoying new experiences while discovering so much more of our great state.

Some might be surprised to find that I hadn't ridden the bike since my Washington to Wisconsin journey during the summer of 2017. That ride ended in July, and the bike received no attention afterwards except some brief preparation for this new adventure. Most of my gear will be the same except I need to be prepared for the cold and damp, both of which I expect to experience. The tent won't go this time because I plan to stay at some of the older motels and take a more relaxed approach. Often, I push the pace considerably but that won't be necessary this time. Nothing about this ride will push the distances that I often have on the summer rides, partly because of the shorter daylight hours. Most days of cycling should be over by 5 p.m.

I am so looking forward to the flat terrain, which makes for easier riding, and enjoying my search for lighthouses and long ocean views. There will be no granny gears used on this ride. Neither will I have to worry about slipping off the back of the seat as I climb huge mountains. The wind might hold me back but I should get some great tailwinds, too. Supply points will likely be frequent so no super large and heavy loads should strain my panniers or my legs.

My clothing will likely continue to consist primarily of shorts and lightweight shirts, at least I hope it will. I plan to pack my long sleeve shirts, a least one of which is wool, and my favorite raincoat so they are ready to go. All the usual tools will ride along again as well as $CO_2$ cartridges and extra tubes. I plan to take Patsy McBride's angel and the famous spoon and fork from my summer ride for good luck along with plenty of prayers from the community.

Just as on my previous cycling adventures, I am expecting my Rowan County family and friends and Salisbury Post readers to go with me. Those suggestions offered are often some of the keys to my successful rides but just knowing that readers are following along matters to me, too. I have received much guidance on where to stay, what to see, the best places to eat and sometimes even directional tips. That input matters and enhances everything I do. Many of the folks who have offered suggestions became friends afterwards, and what could be better than that?

At the end of my travel day to Morehead City, I found a good deal on a motel and walked around some in the Atlantic Beach area as rain continued to pound down. When arriving at the beach, I had only a basic plan to ride north on the "Inland Banks" and was open to any changes perceived as a better choice. My basic plan to start left out plenty of details but I was not worried. My only real concern was that early darkness limited my emergency plan.

## The riding begins

The first thing I did on that Friday was to leave my truck at the Trinity Center in Salter Path. Thanks to my new friend, Mickie, I knew that my truck would be safe when I returned nine or ten days later. Just as my luck would have it, the north wind was cold and I would be cycling into the worst of that. My cycling started off with a ride back to Atlantic Beach and into Morehead City before turning north on N.C. 101 toward Beaufort. The road was good with lessening traffic until a turn onto N.C. 306 took me on a secluded five-mile road to the first ferry of the adventure. I love ferry rides and would hopefully enjoy plenty of them.

My first physical challenge came when I turned onto the road to the ferry with just 30 minutes to go before the next departure. I quickly decided that I couldn't make that five-mile distance in time, but as the minutes passed by, I pushed harder and harder and was surprised to pull onto the ferry ramp just as it was closing up. I made it, a good start, by just about 10 seconds! My alternative would have been to wait an hour for the next ferry.

My dilemma had been to find a quality, detailed North Carolina map that highlighted the coastal area. I found one at the ferry office and now had the means to figure out all the little roads that would enhance the journey. After exiting the ferry, I turned onto N.C. 306 into Arapahoe, followed the Neuse River for a while and then turned toward Oriental, a really cool little town. A high-end sailboat and yacht community on the banks of the Pamlico Sound and the Intracoastal Waterway, Oriental had lots of little shops that looked inviting. I asked about a motel, just for kicks, and was told, "There is nothing here but upper-class lodging. You won't find anything cheap." It didn't matter as I didn't plan to stay in Oriental anyway. It was still a chilly afternoon but I found a convenience store with a few good buys and conversation, too.

Oriental got its name from the sailing steamer that was used as a troop transport early in the Civil War. It ran aground nearby, and legend has it that the postmaster found the ship's nameplate and proposed it as the town's new name.

I pedaled on to Bayboro, where I found one of the coolest lodgings ever experienced in all my travels. I had called the Bayboro Inn earlier and spoken to Gus McDonald, a transplanted Scottish-born American citizen. We negotiated a good rate for a huge upstairs room in the old hotel. Gus was great fun to talk to upon arrival and had plenty of travel stories to share himself. The room and hotel had all the amenities that I needed. Plus the room had three beds, a fireplace and was incredibly spacious. The inn reminded me a little of some of the huge older churches where I had spent the night on previous cycling trips.

Once checked in, I rode down the street to find some batteries and food and got back after dark on a night that was already turning much colder. The wind was still blowing and was expected to continue all night. I was glad to have good heat in the very large room. My heavier clothes would come in handy on Saturday. I stayed warm overnight although I never could get the electric fireplace to work. Speaking of the fireplace, I noticed some movement behind the glass and spotted a very small mouse, which ran back and forth under a door that I suspected was a connector to the next room. I sent an email to the owner later and told him about the mouse, adding that it hadn't really bothered me. A few shoes thrown in his direction didn't even come close.

Heading north from Bayboro, I found Grantsboro first. My fellow summer riders would have termed Grantsboro a real town as it had both a McDonald's and a Walmart. Turning north again on N.C. 306, I pushed on toward Aurora. The days were so short that the sun was already setting as I joined N.C. 32 and then kept pedaling toward Plymouth and the intersection with U.S. 64. I got a great deal on a room at the Rodeway Inn and was glad to get inside with the heat already running. I turned it up even higher. A quick check on the weather forecast brought the good news that the weather was supposed to moderate over the next few days. A long cold day that never made it out of the 40s had left me a sore and stiff cyclist for the first time on this trip.

After a hot shower, I finally felt warm for the first time all day. I had stopped by the office and talked to Nicole, the desk clerk, about my upcoming trip. It was my first real conversation since the evening before, and I missed that part of the daily interaction with locals. Cold people didn't mind talking but only for shorter periods. The chilly wind made just being outside uncomfortable today. I hoped that possibilities for good conversations would follow in the up-coming days.

Up at dawn, I rode toward downtown Plymouth on a chilly morning with no wind, which was a pleasant relief. My first destination was the waterfront and the historic buildings on Water Street. Beautiful views of the Roanoke River caught my attention, followed by the replica of the Roanoke River Lighthouse that was first used in 1866. While the first lighthouse had been anchored in the water, the current one sits firmly on land. I saw announcements of upcoming events centered in the downtown area.

During the Civil War, a fort in town was held by Union troops until the Confederates captured it in April of 1864. Residents in town hid in a nearby house that still remains, complete with bullet holes. A memorial honors all who died, soldiers and civilians alike.

I found Plymouth to be a very cool town with plenty of historical houses and buildings. It also claims to be the home of the last two world record black bears. I had visited Glidden, Wisconsin, during the summer ride, and the residents' fascination with large black bears was quite similar. One of their world record bears was the focus of a replica display and plenty of T-shirts and signs.

On a Sunday morning much more pleasant than the previous day, I left Plymouth, singing hymns on my way out. Things were looking up as I got plenty of waves from the few cars on the road while passing through Roper and Pleasant Grove. Next would come the scenic ride of at least three miles over the Albemarle Sound, where I found wind not to be an issue. On my previous ride over this bridge on the Atlantic Coast journey of 2014, I wondered if I was going to get blown off it. The guardrails are very low, and the wind forced me to move away from the edges of the bridge. I wondered if any cyclists had ever been blown off it.

I passed by on the outskirts of Edenton, a town that I had visited on that earlier trip. I wanted to follow U.S. 17 North to go see Hertford. I knew the town had a one-of-a-kind S bridge crossing over the Perquimans River, and I found it quickly. The bridge was really shaped like a lazy S. A less than busy drawbridge was not manned, and I wondered how often a big boat or ship requires it to be raised.

Hertford's website mentioned that the town seemed to

be from a much easier paced era. I had never seen so many historic homes clustered in such a small town. The oldest brick home in the state was located nearby and was still open for tours, although I didn't try to go find it. The main reason I wanted to visit Hertford, other than the fact that I had never seen it before, was to see how the town had honored Jim "Catfish" Hunter, a Hall of Fame pitcher for the New York Yankees and Oakland A's. Hunter had been the first free agent in major league baseball after signing with the Yankees. He had pitched a perfect game but sadly died at a very young age of Lou Gehrig's Disease, also known as ALS (Amyotrophic Lateral Sclerosis). Hertford had honored Hunter with a memorial on the Town Green and by naming a street beside the local high school and a bridge on U.S. 17 after him.

With almost no wind and thickening clouds coming in, I rode on into Elizabeth City, where I planned to spend the evening. Along the way, I saw plenty of farming going on, much of it to do with cotton. Large cotton bales, many rolled in plastic, had been placed along the roads. Other farmers were harvesting soybeans in wet fields just ahead of the rain forecasted for this night. The brake cable for my back brakes broke, which was not a big deal for such flat land. I could easily stop the bike with one set of brakes working. I noticed the strong smell of wood smoke, possibly from burning brush or heating against the chill.

I chose the Econolodge because of its good price and

fantastic central location. A Burger King was located just across from the motel, and I ordered two very tasty veggie burgers. Virginia was close, but I was now pointed east with a ride on N.C. 158 before turning south to follow the Currituck Sound. The Outer Banks were close but another ride in the rain was expected on Monday. I didn't want to miss a thing along the way.

The weather guy on TV mentioned a front coming through that would bring rain into the area. He seemed to be sure the worst of it would be over by 9 a.m. with the sun coming out later in the day. I wanted to head east, then south all the way to Kitty Hawk, my starting point for Outer Banks exploration.

Leaving Elizabeth City was easy, thanks to great directions from the motel staff. I just made it across the Pasquotank River bridge ahead of the barricades coming down and the drawbridge going up. I stopped in the light rain and watched the drawbridge rise and the boat pass by, and as usual, was quite amazed. Initially, as the rain remained light, I had enough shoulder to stay out of the traffic lanes. Little towns like Belcross, Barco, Grandy and Powell's Point combined with several long sections of morning scenery to make for a pleasant ride. Later, the rain was quite heavy and the temperature was in the mid-40s, making for a cold ride. I had my mittens on, and they were soaked, causing my fingers to feel numb. I stopped at a 7/Eleven and went in to find the warmth amazing. Standing around outside as the rain pelted down, I came up with the idea of wrapping the mittens with plastic shopping bags. After eating pastries while killing some time, I rode on with the rain still falling and the temperature moderating to 48. My hands began to feel much better. Later as the rain lessened, I thought of changing to lighter gloves and still wrapping them. This made my hands toasty until the sun finally began to peek through.

One final challenge was the ride over the Currituck Sound Bridge with the wind blowing from the north, or my left side. A few gusts pushed me as close to the guardrail as I wanted to be until I could finally exit the other side. Kitty Hawk was just on the other side of the bridge, and it would be my first visit to the Outer Banks in many years. I found the nice visitor's center stocked full of so much reading material that it was almost overwhelming. With the help of the volunteer at the desk, we found several pieces of basic all-inclusive material and a few specific brochures on destinations that I wanted to see. I didn't want to miss a thing, and I was on schedule so far. More than once, my ex-wives have hassled me about wanting to see everything. They had called it a fault, but I don't agree!

Listening to some of the other tourists in the visitors center made me want to go see the Wright Brothers' Memorial before ending the day by finding a room with a working heater. I rode down to the gate and met Park Ranger Mary Crocker, who wasn't at all busy on this nasty day and took time to offer me some pointers. The actual visitor's center at the memorial was under renovation, and we couldn't go see it. A very limited presentation in the gift shop wasn't worth much time, and I went on out to climb up a huge dune to the memorial located on top. It was hard to imagine the Wright Brothers lugging their gliders used for testing up that dune and flying off into the same gusty and cold north wind that I faced on this day. They had lived and worked on the plane in small wooden buildings 114 years before. Replicas of those buildings were quite fascinating. The brothers flew the plane on four successful flights on Dec. 17, 1903. The starting points and distances of each flight are marked on the runway with the fourth and longest flight lasting 59 seconds while staying aloft for 852 feet.

After leaving Ranger Crocker a second time, I rode to the Cavalier Inn, one of the oldest motels on the beach. I had an oceanfront room, meaning that I could step into the sand just about 10 feet from my door. The waves themselves were 120 feet away and rolling heavy and hard with the north wind. My goal was to stay in the older "mom and pop" motels for the rest of my visit on the Outer Banks. While checking in, I met a WW II veteran who had visited the motel most of the years since the war and always tried to stay in the same room. It was too cold to sit outside any longer, although I saw a couple next to me doing just that while wrapped in blankets. I went inside and started drying my clothes. Having covered about 230 miles so far, I expected to more than double that number by the trip's end.

I enjoyed a wonderful restful night in the Cavalier by the Sea and was raring to go toward Corolla when I woke up on Tuesday morning. Right away, I was knocked back by hearing the even stronger winds blowing, still from the north. I saw an American flag straining against a huge flagpole and knew that unless something changed, this would be a very hard day. My morning ride would be about 30 miles toward Duck and Corolla into the teeth of that wind. The ride took almost four and a half hours, making the trip very slow, just a little more than six miles an hour.

The first town I came to was Duck, one of the Outer Banks signature towns, with plenty of shops and water sports. Duck also had a decent bike path that ran right beside N.C. 12, the main road. Workers were putting in new ramps to better cross the side streets. I just stayed on the side of the road.

Friends back home had touted Duck Donuts, and I figured what better time to stop and sample them than while the wind was hammering away. The actual store in Duck was still closed about half the days during the off-season, so I would have to find them in other year-round stores.

Despite the long "against the wind" battle, I finally made it to Corolla and went directly to the Currituck Beach Light Station, where I immediately met the site manager, Meghan Agresto. I was pushing my bike onto the walkway between the lighthouse and several other buildings. She told me and another cyclist that we could park our bikes back near the bike stand. Trusting her that nobody would mess with it, Meghan and I eventually went to her office where we discussed the real scoop on Duck Donuts and how to elect better politicians.

I climbed Meghan's lighthouse, totally enjoying the experience except when I went out the door at the top and thought the wind would blow me away. The view was amazing if I could just hold on. The Currituck Lighthouse was the last major one built on the Outer Banks and continues to work until this day. Nearby were the restored keeper's house along with a smaller version, which now served as a gift shop. Even the privy had been restored.

The complex included a bunch of other interesting sights. One was the smallest public school in North Carolina in a restored building that is part of the historic Corolla Village. Children from kindergarten through eighth grade can now attend school locally instead of taking a 90-minute bus ride to other schools across the Currituck Sound. On the day that I was at the school, 34 children were being taught by four teachers. It was cool to see them all outside the building that afternoon.

My other goal for the day was to see the Corolla wild horses. Meghan told me where I might see them, and I also stopped to talk with a deputy sheriff who told me he hadn't seen them that day but that they have about 11 miles to roam between Corolla and the Virginia state line. I never saw the horses, but will save that for another time.

The still gusting breeze pushed me back to the Kitty Hawk area in a little over two hours, less than half the time of the ride north that morning. With darkness on its way, I rode south on U.S. 12 next to the dunes and was amazed at how much sand had blown across the road during the latest storm. I saw several motels that were closed for the season and kept looking as the wind pushed me farther south.

Although the weather was only slightly better on this Tuesday than it was yesterday, I stopped at a Dairy Queen for a small pineapple milkshake. I ordered a small one because of the lingering cold. Just a few blocks away, I stopped at a still open bike shop, where the owners let me oil my chain for free. Just down the street was the Cavalier by the Sea motel, so I decided to stay there again. This time, I took the economy room facing N.C. 12 instead of the ocean.

The Cavalier by the Sea was built in 1949 and is one of the best motels I have stayed in over all my adventure trips. Only twice in my memory have I stayed in the same motel for two straight nights, with the other time being in Williams, Arizona, where I took a train ride to visit the Grand Canyon. Upon check in, I enjoyed a slice of cake that really hit the spot. I was already thinking of heading south the next morning, again with the wind to my back. After submitting my story for the day, I set about planning how to make the most of my day between Kill Devil Hills and Manteo. Of the 29 sights on the must-see list for the

Outer Banks, 12 were on Roanoke Island. I couldn't see them all this Wednesday, but I planned to get to as many as I could. There were no complaining ex-wives close by, at least I hoped not.

First thing on my agenda for the next day was finding the nearest Duck Donuts. I was amazed that it was only 0.3 miles from the Cavalier by the Sea. I was excited to see what was so special about these donuts. Sharon Ritchie from home had mentioned that I had better not miss them. Duck Donuts has about a dozen specially themed toppings. My choices on this day included a blueberry something, a French toast one and a pumpkin variation. With only three donuts ordered, my order was smaller than most but I still got the same size box as those who had ordered a dozen. I ate two of them while they were still hot, after which I definitely experienced a sugar rush, and rated them very highly.

I went the wrong way in search of Jockey's Ridge State Park, but was able to find it with the help of cellphone directions. The park has the highest sand dunes in the United States, and hang gliding is taught there on a daily basis. The high winds must have been an issue because the instructor actually left the park as I was riding in. The park's visitor center was quite interesting and powered totally by a wind generator.

Next I visited the best built pier that I had ever seen, Jeannette's Pier at Nag's Head. It had been built and rebuilt many times because of severe weather but is now operated by North Carolina Aquariums. Just inside the door, I saw a large aquarium and several smaller ones. Part of the facility was used for teaching. Wind generators also power the pier and were spinning especially hard on this day.

Within sight of the pier was U.S. 64, the main road to Roanoke Island and Manteo. I asked to make sure that I had the right idea about cycling over the bridges to Manteo, and was a bit surprised to hear one of the pier staff express concern about me doing this. Compared to other trips involving bridges, this one was very tame but I could see that on certain days, the wind would be a real issue. On this day, however, it was just fine.

My first stop in Manteo was the waterfront and the Roanoke Marshes Lighthouse. The wonderful boardwalk around the marina was really cool with sailboats tied up alongside it. Waterfront Manteo is chockfull of cool little shops and stores and couldn't be prettier. I could see the Elizabeth II across the marina, but didn't know how to get there. A little later, I saw a couple of cyclists pedaling over the waterway bridge and followed them.

On the other side of the bridge was the fabulous Roanoke Island Festival Park. The park includes the Elizabeth II, a replica sailing ship of the type used by the English when colonists were brought to this area. An authentic English village and Indian settlement are also on site. A wonderful museum included all the major happenings of the island, including the Lost Colony, Fort Raleigh, a Civil War battle, a freedmen's settlement, early radio transmissions and of course, pirates. There was just so much to see that I am sure I missed listing something.

Next was the Manteo Airport, where I had a mission to fulfill. Marianne Wilson of Landis had contacted me about stopping to see the Civil Air Patrol Museum at the airport and told me that her dad, Lt. Otho Corriher, served there during World War II. As a huge history nut, I was amazed by the efforts of civilian pilots in underpowered Piper Cubs who flew off the coast looking for German submarines. As part of the war effort, pilots brought their own planes to spot the subs and inform military units in the area. Those submarines played havoc with Allied shipping during the first part of the war, but were almost totally eradicated due to the civilian pilots' efforts. Corriher served from 1942 to 1943 and received a Presidential Commendation for his efforts. His name was listed on a monument outside the main building of the airport.

Also just outside the airport was the first monument I had seen to honor the freedmen's colony. With the Union victories in the area, word spread that freedom for slaves was available on the island. Many of the slaves worked for and eventually enlisted in the U.S. Army during the last two years of the war, while many of their families still live in the area.

Not far from the airport was the Fort Raleigh National Park, site of the Lost Colony settlement and a small earthen fort where the Civil War battle was fought. After touring the visitor center and watching a movie concerning the history of the area, I took the nature walk that included both of these sites. Especially interesting was the outdoor theatre used for the Lost Colony presentation each summer.

As the day slipped away, I had to find a place to stay. I called a couple of places and wasn't especially excited about what I heard. "Just for grins," as my nephew would say, I stopped at the Elizabethan Inn back in town. While it looked quite expensive from outside, I took a chance and went inside to tell my story. I had a nice talk with the manager and ended up with a wonderful price on a room. Food was available close by at a convenience store and so ended my "see everything possible in a day" portion of the trip. I had plenty of planning to do for the next few days. More lighthouses would be coming up!

After a mostly quiet night, I pedaled back over to U.S. 64 and headed east to rejoin N.C. 12. Back to the mostly quiet night, I got in the room before dark, and all was quiet until the continued thumping noises next door sounded like someone was rearranging the room for about an hour. There was lots of bumping, banging and loud steps. Just before I headed back to the desk to complain, the sound of silence returned and thankfully, remained for the rest of the night. There were very few vehicles parked at the motel that night, so the noise could have come from motel staff workers doing something.

With all that behind me, I made a beeline for the 7/Eleven at the intersection of U.S. 64 and N.C. 12. The best thing about the stop was that several people asked about my bike ride. One of them was quite interesting himself. Harry Veihmeyer had a kayak strapped to the top of his car and said he planned to use it for fishing all the way from the Dry Tortugas south of Key West up the east coast of North America to Newfoundland. He asked me to share tips on keeping his electronics charged and how to find good places to stay.

This was going to be my day for lighthouses, and I was headed directly for the Bodie Island version. Early in the morning, I found it looking quite spectacular against the clear blue sky. The Bodie Island Lighthouse has been built and rebuilt two more times since the original structure went up. At 150 feet tall, the name is pronounced more like "body," and legend has it that many bodies had washed ashore in the area following shipwrecks.

Heading south, I entered Cape Hatteras National Seashore and found a huge amount of sand being cleaned off the road by large dirt-moving equipment. Often, I rode on a thin layer of sand along the edge of the pavement. The most amazing thing I saw that morning was the size of the new Oregon Inlet Bridge. It dwarfs the old bridge that it will replace, and construction equipment was being moved about on barges pushed by tugboats. Supplies and huge cranes moved back and forth on the water, and I got great pictures while watching from a closed construction lane.

My Thursday morning ride was more pleasant because the weather had improved. A gentle wind blew under a bright sun with gradually warming temperatures. I saw a large number of dead deer, raccoons and other roadkill in the area, making me wonder if some of them had died in the flooding that moved all the sand.

Just past this area was the Pea Island Wildlife Refuge. I have never seen nor heard so many birds in my life. Hundreds of bird species can be seen in the 13-mile stretch of riding that had little else. I was amazed that so many birds seemed to feel safe in the area. I stopped to check out a small museum at the refuge and found it quite interesting.

Next on my trip was Rodanthe, another town that I had learned to pronounce correctly. One of my goals was to find the house that had been used in the 2008 movie, "Nights in Rodanthe," starring Diane Lane and Richard Gere. The volunteer at the wildlife refuge told me how to identify the house, unusual in that it was the first house with blue shutters.

A small sign confirmed the fact that the house was in fact the famous one and that it had been moved off the beach. Now available for rent, the sign also reminded people like me that the house was private property.

Also in Rodanthe was possibly the best stop of a whole day of great stops. I was especially interested in seeing the Chicamacomico Life Saving Station, which is historically significant and includes a wonderful museum. With so many people losing their lives from shipwrecks along the Outer Banks coast, the federal government authorized a service allowing men to train together for the sole purpose of saving as many people as possible. All this started in 1874, and this particular station was the most notable of more than 100 in all. Many of them still remain and are now used as residences or small businesses.

The museum and grounds are spectacular, and I could have spent a whole day there looking in all the buildings. All of them were close to being historically accurate. A fully stocked circa-1900 house and the living quarters for the men of the life saving service were jammed full of interesting things to see. Elaine Haines was about as good as a tour guide can be as she gently pointed me toward touring the grounds in the correct order.

I also met Marilyn Boyleston from just south of Erie, Pennsylvania. She visits the area nearly every year and was heading south, where she planned to end her day at the Cape Hatteras Lighthouse, just the same as me. We both wanted to take a sunset photo.

Avon was the next town I went through and then it was on to Buxton, the home of the next lighthouse. The Cape Hatteras Lighthouse is the tallest brick lighthouse in North America at 208 feet. Its light can be seen from 20 miles out to sea and several miles from town. After missing the correct turnoff, I had to double back and find the lighthouse

164

even though I had seen it often as I approached Buxton. As the sun moved lower in the sky, I found my way into the museum area. The museum, which I had been told was one of the best, was closed, but the gift shop was open. The keeper's house, doubling as the museum, was closed because of lack of available staff. Yet, they had a handful of people in an almost empty gift shop.

It was amazing to see two great lighthouses in the same day, and I got some amazing photos with the sun behind the Cape Hatteras Lighthouse as it set. Now that darkness was quickly approaching, I had to find a place to stay, and the first place I called was too high. I received a tip to try the Cape Pines Motel, built in the late 1940s and located just across the street from a busy and well-stocked grocery store. The desk clerk was wonderful, and I soon had a room and plenty of food. I enjoyed a very restful night in another nearly perfect room.

Just two days of riding remained as I awoke on Friday morning. The wind was blowing hard, and the cold was back, at least for the day. I was sad to leave the comfortable Cape Pines Motel. Though I had gone back to wearing multiple layers of clothes, including long pants, the wind was mostly behind my back, always a pleasant thing.

I found a sign at the local bookstore to be very interesting as it was promoting the latest book by Joseph C. Ellis, who just happens to be my mentor on writing books. Joe, who is from Ohio, and I got to know each other because we are both runners and he sent me a book to read pre-publication. It was quite good, and we struck up a friendship that allowed me to ask many pertinent questions about how to write a book and get it published. Most of Joe's books are about murder on the Outer Banks in some way, and they are quite popular. The latest is titled "Murder in Ocracoke," and it features the Ocracoke Lighthouse, which I planned to see later that day.

Farther south, I passed through Frisco and spotted an alien spacecraft, complete with waving operators. Nobody else seemed worried about the otherworldly craft, so I took a couple of photos and again kept riding.

Hatteras was next, where I spotted a bakery that was open and ready for business. Many businesses had already closed for the winter season. Traffic was very light as well, probably the lightest of the whole trip. After picking up a few things at the bakery, I headed over to the U.S. Weather Bureau Station. Constructed in 1901, the station collected weather data until the 1940s and was later renovated as the town's visitor center. One brochure said that the Wright Brothers got their weather information from these stations.

The visitor center operator told me about a nearby shipwreck that was sometimes visible. I went in search of the shipwreck but didn't find it. The sea was calm but near high tide.

My last stop in Hatteras was the Graveyard of the Atlantic Museum, one of the best museums that I have ever seen. Complete with fantastic exhibits on shipwrecks, deep sea diving, the ironclad USS Monitor and other Civil War Naval actions, commercial fishing and plenty about pirates, it would have taken at least a whole day here, too, to see everything. I stayed two hours and will definitely return to the free museum at a later date.

Just next door was the loading area for the start of the hour-long ferry ride to Ocracoke. This ferry had a special place for bicycle riders to wait. The workers loaded the bikes last but it didn't take long. I stayed at the museum until about 10 minutes before loading and timed it just right. The ferry is the only way to make the trip to Ocracoke, other than by small plane.

The ferry ride took about an hour, and I was soon standing on the island of Ocracoke, which is about 15 miles long. Most of the first 13 miles is a straight shot through high dunes on both sides of the road. Much of the time, I couldn't see the ocean. About six miles from the ferry was the pony pen, the area where the Ocracoke ponies are now kept behind fences. After missing the Corolla horses on the other end of the Outer Banks, I did only slightly better at the pony pen with just a few of the horses spotted in distant corrals.

While I was there, workers with the National Park Service and AmeriCorps were building a deck of sorts on a storage area which was part of the pony pasture. I was told that the ponies would not be able to roam freely until later in the day or after the work was finished, so my distant pictures would have to do. The ponies, descended from Spanish horses, are often called "banker ponies" and were used by the Coast Guard and the Lifesaving Service that I mentioned earlier.

My evening was going to be spent in Ocracoke, but I did not know where. I stopped at the Bluff Shoals Motel and was told that all rooms were full. I checked at the Blackbeard Lodge and walked all through the place without finding anyone. After checking a couple more places, I returned to the Bluff Shoals, where I got a special deal on an apartment for the night. I could see the lighthouse from the apartment.

Before the end of the day, I wanted to ride over and find the Ocracoke Lighthouse for some close-up pictures. The lighthouse appears to be on private property and is not open to the public, although there is a boardwalk to it. I then rode through some of the older sections of town and out to the ferry landing, from which I planned to depart early the next morning. Imagine my surprise to see that the sun was about to set in the Pamlico Sound, all the way to the water and nothing was in the way!

I waited for the sunset and made some of the most spectacular pictures ever, just as good as the ones I had taken in Key West. Just five minutes later, I could see the light shining from the lighthouse. I was reminded that exactly 300 years ago on this very day, Friday, Nov. 17, Blackbeard captured the ship that would become his flagship, Queen Anne's Revenge. Blackbeard has been mentioned often during the Outer Banks portion of this ride.

The early ferry ride this morning would take me to Cedar Island and a resumption of N.C. 12, after which I plan to follow U.S. 70 back toward Morehead City and Salter Path, where my truck was parked. I didn't sleep really well last night for some reason and got up at 5 a.m. even though I didn't need to. The ferry ride was only about a half mile away and was leaving at 7:30 a.m. I did have to be on that departure to make my goal of reaching Salter Path today.

With some extra time on my hands, I cleaned the apartment and bagged up all the trash. I also added air to both bike tires for the first time since Day 1. I had caught up on my email and text messages and ended up leaving a half hour early to meet the ferry. Just down the street, my front tire went flat even though just minutes before, it appeared to be holding air just fine. I pumped it up again by CO2 cartridge and it seemed OK. The flat tire was probably caused by some type of operator error.

I was especially excited about the ferry ride, this time on the biggest and most modern ferry that I had ever seen. My fee to ride was $3, a bargain since I was going to be on the ferry for over two hours. Once again, I waited until the last cars were on the ferry and walked my bike on. There was plenty of room this time with only a dozen or so cars on this early Saturday morning ride. I went upstairs and found an amazing passenger lounge, large and comfortable with wonderful views and seats high above the water. For the $3 fee, I got all this plus a dolphin sighting. The Pamlico Sound was as smooth as glass when we cast off and not much worse when we landed. With nothing to do but relax, I greatly enjoyed this part of the adventure.

Back on solid ground, I had some serious pedaling to do. My goal was to be back at the Trinity Center Camp and Conference Retreat, where my truck was parked, by 3 p.m. After the 23 miles by boat, I had 52 to do by bike against a stiffening headwind and building traffic. Mickie Whitley had been watching my truck at the Trinity Center, and I wanted to see her before she left work.

So the pedaling began back at Cedar Island, a sparsely populated wildlife refuge area. I passed through lots of very small towns like Atlantic, Stacy, Davis, Williston and Smyrna. I had several changes in direction that helped with the wind but the closeness to the water and the open area seemed to enhance it.

Beaufort was the first real town I encountered, and it had the worst roads and traffic. There was so little room to ride, causing me to miss the wide-open areas of the smaller towns. Beaufort also had the last big bridge to pedal over and it did not have any bike lanes, making the crossing fairly tight. I managed not to get buzzed, the feeling that happens when a mirror just misses my elbow. I'm not sure whether Beaufort or Morehead City actually owned the bridge.

Once I had officially arrived in Morehead City, the roads widened and traffic lessened on the way to the causeway and another good-sized bridge that served as the entrance to Atlantic Beach. I was back where I had spent the first night of the adventure. The ride and final push on Fort Macon Road that became Salter Path Road was very friendly with wide bike lanes and mostly flat riding. I pedaled hard in this segment and hit the entrance to the Trinity Center at 3:08 p.m., the time when the official bike ride ended. I met Mickie and gave her one of my newest books. She offered a room and graciously invited me to come back at another time. I will take her up on that. Can't wait!

With such a beautiful afternoon to enjoy and almost two hours until dark, I wanted to visit nearby Fort Macon. After having visited the area several times, I wanted to stop this time and tour the fort. Fort Macon is owned by the State of North Carolina, and there is an awesome presentation of history in place there. The fort was used in the Spanish-American War, by both sides in the Civil War and by the U.S. Military during World War II. There were very detailed exhibits of all of these, especially the Civil War times, and looking at them took me well past sunset. I could have stayed much longer but I felt that someone would eventually run me out. The main visitor center had closed, but all the individual rooms in the fort were still wide open at dark. Most of the rooms held such interesting exhibits that plenty of people were still touring them.

Lee and Tricia Johnson had arranged to let me use their condo, located just a half mile from the Trinity Center, for my final night along the coast. Dr. Johnson is my urologist, while Tricia and I have worked on several races together. This was a perfect wind-down to a wonderful nine days and just over 500 miles, counting ferry rides, along the Inner and Outer Banks of North Carolina. The scenery was magnificent, the history amazing and the people were just what I had hoped for. Genuine, realistic and friendly!

Many friends have asked why I chose to go in the off season. My answer was that the lighter traffic, lower motel prices and reasonable temperatures all were in my favor with much more room for the bike. Once again, the prayers and suggestions of readers had made the trip successful. Thanks for riding along, and let's go again soon!

The start

Winding Stair Gap

Bridal Veil Falls

Manure spreader

Sunset Motel

Cape Hatteras Lighthouse in the mountains

Miniature horses and burro

Freeze's daughter Amber in Morganton

Wayne Collins of Connelly Springs

David and Amy Frazier

Randy Stewart's racing go kart

Horses near home

179

Heavy snow east of Lexington

Loading up on doughnuts

Aunt Bee's grave

Tim and William Deal

Another police stop

Natalie Newcomb of Lucama

James and Beatrice Mullins of Pinetops

Alligator River Lighthouse

Lindsay Warren Bridge

The finish at Whalebone Junction

The run across North Carolina is official.

Celebrating the achievement

Easy pedalling on the Outer Banks

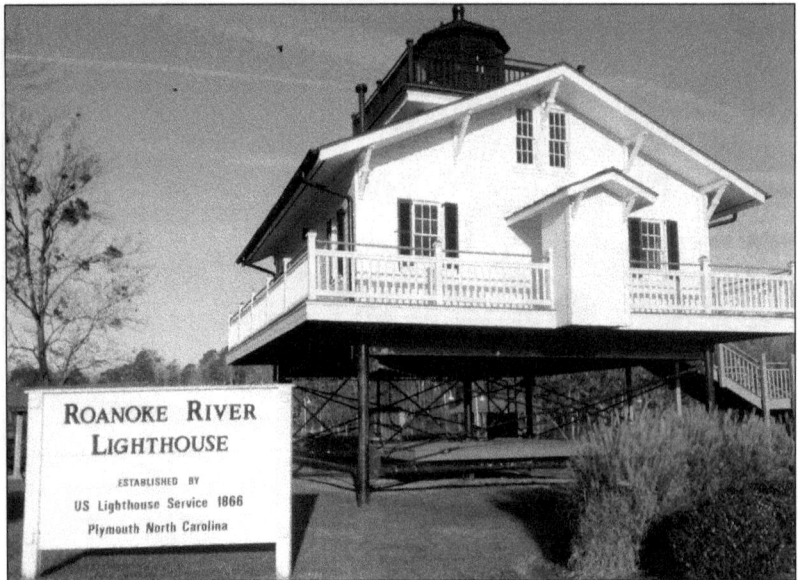

Roanoke River Lighthouse in Plymouth

186

S bridge in Hertford

Wright Brothers Memorial

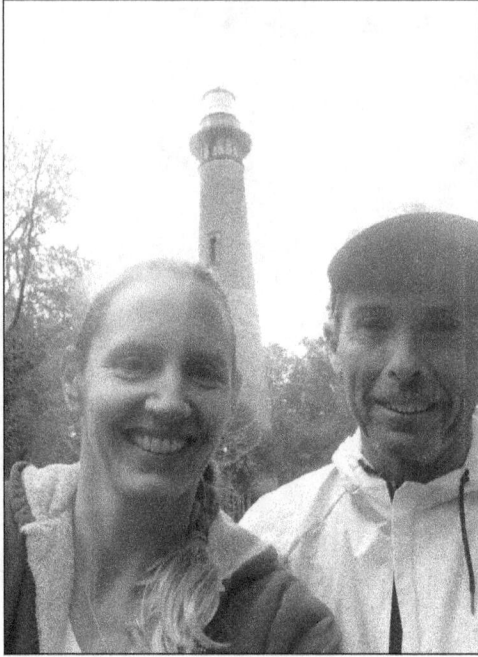

Meghan
Agresto
and the
Currituck
Island
Lighthouse

Elizabeth II

Bodie Island Lighthouse

Chicamacomico Lifesaving Station

Cape Hatteras Lighthouse

Alien spacecraft

Ocracoke Lighthouse

Ocracoke/Pamlico Sound sunset

# EPILOGUE

*One day at a time!*

. . . . . . . . . . . . . . . . . . . . . . . . . . . . . . . . . . . . . . . . . . . . . . . . . .

After my visit with Ed Dupree in our local hospital in September of 2016, I couldn't put the idea of this first major journey on foot out of my mind. To begin with, I was already busy with plans for another bike ride and knew virtually nothing about covering a long multi-day distance like this on foot. Ed Dupree probably knew that I would become focused on all the intricacies of how to pull off more than 600 miles behind a baby jogger. Of course, Ed would have planned the trip in a different way. For me, it all came together and the telling of it in this book covered a host of wonderful memories.

I remember being ready and busting to go as we drove the last miles to the start. My emotions at saying good-bye to my daughter, Amber, and her fiancee, Jamie, surprised me, and I had no idea of how many more emotions I would go through as my trip progressed. My mind was overcome with possibilities as I stood at the Tennessee state line ready to run. The Atlantic Ocean seemed so very far away.

As always, certain challenges remain fresh in my memories. The snow in Highlands and later in Lexington, along with flurries on several other days, was more fun than hindrance. The cold temperatures dipping as low as 19 degrees weren't a big deal either even though the original 10-day forecast had changed dramatically. This comes from a guy who usually can't stand cold weather. The chilling temperatures and blowing snow on the way to Morganton, requiring me to use the Hot Hands packets, stood out more because of the answered prayer that helped me find them. The warm weather of the last few days was greatly appreciated as was the ice cream that I found to finish off some of the better days.

Running on the interstate highway was a surprise because I had no idea it was even allowed in North Carolina. All the law enforcement stops were, at least in my mind, more humorous than anything else. I will admit some frustration after being stopped twice by Raleigh policemen within 20 minutes, and especially with the overly serious tone of the officer on the second one. But still, those men and women were just doing their job, and it was good to have them out there.

Overall, my motel experiences were pleasant and occurred with few problems, except for the Ross Motel in Williamston. Even that one managed to inspire a few extra smiles as I rode away the next morning. I got lost twice in Franklin, and going around a four-mile loop to return to exactly where I had begun was probably my biggest mistake. Nothing to do but laugh about going around in a circle.

Still, I learned from that experience and quickly moved on. A firm bed, a hot shower and good WiFi were all I needed and expected.

People days versus scenery days: that is how I refer to most of my time on the road whether by bike or on foot. The scenery was quite special on this trip and those views of the mountains, especially with the snow, and the Outer Banks just ahead as I reached the top of the nearby bridges stood out. What a great road U.S. 64 is! One day, I hope to return to it and do more in other states.

History, one of my favorite subjects, was found in places that I didn't expect like the Bunker Hill covered bridge and the Revolutionary War memorials along the way to Morganton. Aunt Bee's grave and her jars of pickles in Siler City were very sentimental for me.

Not once on this trip was I really far from help if I had needed it, but there were times with no cell phone coverage. The baby jogger — thanks again to Crystal Karriker! — performed flawlessly and was just one of many godsends along the way. Those plastic-wheeled ones would have probably ended up broken, but who knows? Maybe not. All of my other equipment served its purpose, even though the cyclometer was again challenging until I was able to get it repaired for $1. A big boost came from the inexpensive radio that I bought at Walmart in Murphy. Listening to the weather forecast, along with the hymns and other music to which I sang along, sure helped pass the time on the long days.

Back to the people. I wondered early in the planning process if people would be as involved on this trip. It turned out that they were, especially with their curiosity surrounding the baby jogger and the various perceptions of why it was slowly heading east across our great state. I was not transporting a baby and was not homeless, nor was I especially cold. All of those were reasons why motorists regularly stopped to check on me, demonstrating the goodness of people in general. By now, you have read the stories of Nicole, Courtney, Tia and William, plus so many more. I will always wonder about Julie from Chimney Rock and where she is today. It was fun to think about my college friends whose towns I passed through on the road and wonder where they were now and how their lives had developed. On this adventure, the people I met overwhelmed the scenery. But honestly, I think that has always been the case.

Tim and William Deal, Wayne Crowder, my daughter Amber, and all those folks who took time to find me on the road as I passed through were much appreciated and a big boost to my trip.

I experienced some soreness and tenderness as my body got used to a pace that totaled more than a marathon a day, something that I had no thoughts of accomplishing until the last week of the journey. Food and plenty of it mattered, and I found good sources of supply. The rumble strips that forced me and the baby jogger either off the road or into the traffic lane were not appreciated but I guess they do serve a purpose. Vehicle drivers took care of me and provided plenty of room although I wonder just how often they were influenced by the baby jogger itself. Logging trucks also gave me room, sometimes just enough, and thankfully, the alligators and bears didn't show.

Cycling seems supersonic to me after the roughly four miles per hour pace of this adventure from the mountains to the sea. I was often short on food and water with long miles to go. But never was I short of excitement and the sense of adventure. Hymns and prayers, tears and fist pumping, all played a part and especially highlighted the last few days.

I believe Ed Dupree would have been happy with my version of crossing North Carolina on foot. We both probably enjoyed the "found money" quest way too much. I felt Ed's presence with me often and especially as I neared the end. In closing, I am particularly glad you took the time to run/walk along with Ed and me.

The plans are already at work for another adventure. Join me again soon!

# ABOUT THE AUTHOR

After multiple long distance solo cycling adventures, a new type of challenge was completed with the run/walk across North Carolina. The realization and compilation of this new adventure included not just Freeze's own thoughts but those of a great friend who had recently passed away. This is the author's seventh book, all chronicling travel and adventure of some sort, as well as his compelling interaction with backroads Americans along the way. David Freeze has not been everywhere yet but he's adding to his list. When cycling all 50 states across America are done, what and where will be the next adventure? You can bet he's working on it now.

David is also a motivational speaker, emphasizing that regular people can achieve amazing things. Contact him at david.freeze@ctc.net. Walnut Creek Farm Publishing is named after his farm.

An accomplished runner and endurance cyclist, David has written five other books that cover various adventures across America by bicycle and one by historic biplane. He has completed nearly 84,000 running miles and over 16,000 endurance cycling miles.

*Other books by David Freeze include:*

- **Lord, Ride with Me Today**
  The story of a solo coast-to-coast bicycle journey — 2013

- **Pedaling, Prayers and Perseverance**
  35 Days Cycling Solo from Maine to Key West — 2014

- **Riding the Rails to Freedom**
  Cycling the Underground Railroad Route from Alabama to Ontario — 2015

- **Highway to History**
  A Cycling Adventure on Route 66 — 2016

- **Young Again**
  Veterans recapture a moment of youth through
  Ageless Aviation Dreams Foundation — 2017

- **Cycling the Northwest**
  A solo trip from the West Coast to Green Bay, through
  Bigfoot country — 2017

www.ingramcontent.com/pod-product-compliance
Lightning Source LLC
Chambersburg PA
CBHW072003060426
42446CB00042B/1513